COURAGEOUS
DISCOMFORT

COURA
DISCO

**How to Have Important,
Brave, Life-Changing Conversations
about Race and Racism**

GEOUS
MFORT

20 Questions about Race and Racism Answered

Shanterra McBride and Rosalind Wiseman

CHRONICLE BOOKS
SAN FRANCISCO

To Olivia, who gave me space to write and the perfect breaks to remind me to play. May you always remember that you are marvelous.

To Alice, who showed me the power of love and the pain of racism.

Copyright © 2022 by Shanterra McBride and Rosalind Wiseman.

Library of Congress Cataloging-in-Publication Data is available.

ISBN 978-1-7972-1526-6

Manufactured in China.

Design by Vanessa Dina.
Typesetting by Frank Brayton.
Typeset in TT Ramillas and Noah Grotesque.

10 9 8 7 6 5 4 3 2

Chronicle books and gifts are available at special quantity discounts to corporations, professional associations, literacy programs, and other organizations. For details and discount information, please contact our premiums department at corporatesales@chroniclebooks.com or at 1-800-759-0190.

Chronicle Books LLC
680 Second Street
San Francisco, California 94107
www.chroniclebooks.com

FRIENDS AND RELATIONSHIPS

WORK AND COMMUNITY

However You Got Here, You're in the Right Place

Are you fed up with how people "talk" about race and racism? Are you worried when people use debates about race to prop up their own egos and political ambitions? Are you scared that race is dividing us and blinding us to our shared humanity?

We are too.

Have you ever felt silenced when you've tried to share your thoughts, feelings, or questions about racism?

We can help you.

We are two people who love talking about uncomfortable topics; we've been doing it in our work and in our friendship for over twenty years. We are *friend* friends: We have each other's backs, we start our phone calls without saying hello, we have arguments without saying a word, and we get frustrated with each other, including when we discuss race. Our more-than-twenty-year bond is the inspiration for this book. In fact, it's the reason we *can* write this book, because you can't cowrite a book about race with a person of a different race without seriously trusting them.

This book is for people who want to have more ease in handling the uncomfortable conversations about race that we so often turn away from. But we're going to name the elephant in the room. Well, not just the elephant, the whole zoo: Many of us *seriously* struggle with managing our thoughts and feelings about race and racism, so much so that developing the skills to talk about them honestly and productively feels insurmountable. We worry we'll say the wrong thing. That worry is often the reason why we stumble over our words, laugh awkwardly, or stay silent when someone says something we know is wrong. It's why we make assumptions about others and then shut down when we feel like we have been misunderstood, blamed, or judged.

But we are all harmed by our inability to handle the presence of racism in our lives (and let's be clear: It's present in all of our lives). We all have work to do, and this book will show you how to begin that work and integrate it into your life.

When we began writing this book, we knew what we were doing was important. But we couldn't have imagined that we would write a book like this at a time filled with so much widespread cultural turmoil. We are living at a societal inflection point, one where many are educating or reeducating themselves about how to deal with racism, difference, and a lack of inclusivity in their lives. And attempting to change any ingrained behavior is inherently uncomfortable.

So, we have a choice: We either move toward what makes us uncomfortable so that we better understand our changing world and heal our relationships and communities, or turn away from each other because it feels too threatening and alienating to do the work.

If you are feeling uncomfortable reading these pages, rest assured: We felt uncomfortable writing them. We are right here living through this with you. We have struggled to educate ourselves and to write about what we learned, both alone and together. We have felt overwhelmed. We worried that we wouldn't get it all "right." We have felt anxious and, at times, wondered if it was worth it. But we know it is.

There is a ton of nuance in the topics we'll delve into in this book, but we'll always bring it back to the basics: Every human being should be treated with dignity, and coming together to face our fears instead of allowing our fears to control us is what gets us there.

Whatever brought you here, we believe you are here on purpose to take this journey with us. And we're glad you're here.

Who Are We and
Why Are We Writing This Book?

SHANTERRA

Believe me when I say that I felt the palpable weight of writing this book with the knowledge that I was speaking through a Black woman's lens. In my family, we don't often stumble over words when it comes to talking about race and racism. We don't dance around what we're trying to say because there isn't usually "worry" about saying the wrong thing. I've noticed my family is like a lot of other Black families; what we say in response to racism is because of our past trauma *with* racism. And yes, we can shut down when we feel like we are dismissed, misunderstood, blamed, or judged. Oftentimes, shutting down is easier than trying to convince someone that you may know what you're talking about from your past experiences. That doesn't make it right; it just makes it honest.

I met Rosalind when we worked together shortly after she founded a violence prevention nonprofit for young people in Washington, DC. A week after Rosalind and I started working together, we took a trip to Boston for a conference. I'll never forget getting into the passenger seat of our rental car and Rosalind handing me a paper map and asking me to "lead the way." (Yes, this was before any kind of electronic navigation.) I looked at her seriously and said, "I don't do maps." Without missing a beat, Rosalind busted out laughing, and I couldn't help but do the same. We've been inseparable since.

Rosalind and I talk candidly about the hard, uncomfortable

things. We always have. The conversations haven't always been easy, but they've always been honest.

OK, I know that's nice, but *why* am I (a Black woman) cowriting this book? Why do I feel like I have to add my voice to all the other voices in the room?

For more than twenty-five years, I have partnered with young people to nurture their development. More recently, I feel called to partner with white people, particularly those who want to dismantle racism. Not because they need me to partner with them, but because history has shown us that we do much better working together to end injustice. As a Black woman living in America, finding allies to do that with is a beautiful bonus. However, I also feel called to work with people who don't identify as anti-racist but want to do better, and even those who don't believe racism is a problem.

I remember watching the news one day in January 2019 and seeing a young, white student visiting the Lincoln Memorial with his high school. The next few moments became a cultural flashpoint for the country.

The student was male and wearing a red "Make America Great Again" hat. He reminded me of students I'd had in my years as an assistant principal and traveling the country speaking at schools. A video showing a seeming confrontation between the student and a protester, an older Indigenous man, went viral. There were so many speculations about the encounter, and especially about the student. Different media outlets called the student disrespectful or confrontational even though we never heard the student's voice; we just saw his face. People drew so many conclusions about him, our country, and race relations, from one video clip.

While watching the encounter, I could only think about how I would love to have a conversation with this student. I wanted to give him space to talk about what he was feeling and what he was thinking. I also wanted to see if there were questions about race, identity, and equality that he wanted to ask. Maybe questions that, if asked in a classroom or in the presence of any Black person, Indigenous person, or person of color, would lead him to be labeled a racist even if they were asked out of genuine curiosity. I wanted to talk with him and not judge him.

It was then that I realized that I had been having conversations, mostly with friends who looked like me, *about* the behavior of white people but that I hadn't *included* white people in the conversation except for my close white friends, like Rosalind. Watching the exchange between that high school student and a Native American man and the public debate about what happened between them shifted my conversations. I knew I had to do the work I'd been waiting on someone else to do, not because someone told me to do the work or that, as a Black woman, I should be expected to do the work, but because I felt a personal calling to help end systemic racism.

ROSALIND
My first memory of Shanterra was not of meeting her, it was of hearing about her. One day,

13

my friend and colleague Greg Taylor said to me, "I've just hired someone who should be working with you, and you're going to be best friends for the rest of your life." I was doubtful; I didn't make friends easily, and I was beginning to realize that I was "a lot." Not necessarily in a bad way, but just in an "a lot" way. Despite my doubts, I was very curious. *Who was this person?*

Of course, that person was Shanterra. For years we worked together, and as we did, we built a relationship of trust that allowed us to talk about the topics people usually stay away from. Shanterra was also by my side when one of my books, *Queen Bees and Wannabes*, was published, turned into a bestseller, and shortly thereafter was adapted into the movie *Mean Girls*. For better or worse, that experience changed my life. Overnight, I went from a thirty-one-year-old woman running a local nonprofit (with a newborn) to a national spokesperson on all things parenting, "mean girls," and "mean women." Shanterra was one of the few people I trusted to share how complicated that experience was for me.

Over the years, I moved beyond *Queen Bees* and focused on how to help young people and the adults in their lives treat themselves and others with dignity. Dignity is the guiding principle of my life. Although I have written many books, articles, and curricula that address racism, I never felt I was doing enough, and I knew I was in a position to do more.

As someone who is Jewish, I have often felt the privilege of being white more than of being in a marginalized group. I have experienced anti-Semitism, but not widely; the instances have always felt like isolated events, not a systemized practice meant to dismiss me or deny me opportunities or access. Because my everyday lived experience is almost always that of a white woman, it has often felt like I've been allowed to *choose* to do anti-racist work instead of being obligated to do it because of my being Jewish. As we wrote this book, and especially as attacks against Jewish people escalated throughout the United States, my identity as a Jew hit home, and I've had to reconcile all these painful experiences.

But why write about it now?

Because I am frustrated by watching and listening to people have conversations that reinforce each other's assumptions.

Because I am angry at people in positions of power who divide us for their political and financial gain.

Because I am fed up with the fact that very few of us were, or are, educated about our complex history and the legacy of racism that literally whitewashes and deletes history.

Because I have taught many students of color over the years who have shared their anger about and exhaustion with dealing with the racism of their peers, parents, teachers, coaches, administrators, and institutions.

Because I have faith that people can learn to have hard conversations with one another and see the tremendous benefit that comes from doing so.

And finally, because I want to write a book that doesn't just sit on your bedside table. I want this book to mean something to you and encourage you to have hard conversations and take action in whatever meaningful way you choose.

Who Is This Book for?

This book is meant to speak to white people directly, but not exclusively. We know that white people don't only want to hear what they're doing wrong; they want to hear what they can do right and be empowered and equipped to make a difference.

This book is also for anyone who wants the courage to have uncomfortable conversations about race and racism. To state the obvious: No matter what race you are, you can have complex feelings and beliefs about other people based on their race. People of different races and ethnicities can have negative beliefs and use them to reinforce stereotypes and justify racist actions. That is not exclusive to any one group, culture, or country. And just because it's common doesn't make it right or acceptable. We also know that people, no matter what their race, may also want other ways to approach the painful moments when racism is staring at them through the eyes of another.

We don't speak for everyone, especially the people who have the same or similar outward identities as we do. One of us is Black and Christian and a lot of other things. The other is white and Jewish and a lot of other things. We have done our best to be inclusive enough to make sure every person somehow sees themselves in the words written here.

For people of color, this book may offer some affirmation of your experiences, but you could also disagree with what we have written. Your experiences are your own. This book will ask you to partner with people who aren't the same race or ethnicity as you even though you may have grown up not trusting them, especially if they haven't risen to the occasion in the way you have wanted or expected them to. We don't want to brush over the fact that it is hard to trust people who have disappointed or even betrayed you, or personify a group of people who do. We're asking you to be on a path with us. We acknowledge that the burden is not on people of color to make themselves uncomfortable by partnering with white people in the same way that white people need to make themselves uncomfortable with each other. We are asking you to exhale and see if what we wrote can help move the needle forward.

The Past Is the Prologue to the Present

The concepts in this book are based on a fundamental premise: Despite its founding principles, the United States was built on inequality, injustice, and the genocide of some of its inhabitants. For more than 400 years, our history has been inextricably tied to slavery and, after emancipation in 1865, to laws, policies, and institutions that enforced those policies to make sure that people of color and, more specifically, Black and Indigenous people, would not have equal opportunity. Since then, whenever there is a significant attempt to acknowledge and address this tragedy, powerful forces mobilize to put this history back into the shadows.

You may be thinking and feeling a lot of things at this point. You may agree, be uncertain, or disagree with everything we've written here so far. You may even want to put this book down right now. If you don't agree (*especially* if you don't agree), we ask that you stay with us and keep reading. We know that acknowledging the present-day reality of racism is fundamentally opposite to what we have been taught about our country and what it stands for. We know that many among us think it would be better if we just focused on what brings us together and keep the past in the past. But asking that of people who have been targeted for discrimination and violence because of their race is not only unsafe, it is a fundamental denial of their daily experience and history. For the rest of us, if these efforts that are opposed to education and dialogue are successful, it means that we don't believe in our own (and our children's) capacity, fortitude, and resilience to learn from our past so that we can be capable, critically thinking

people who can face significant challenges.

It comes down to this: If we
believe we are all better off
living in communities where
people can do their best to
thrive and contribute to the
greater good, white people
must begin by acknowledging
the profound sanctity of what
people of color are telling us
is in their hearts and minds.
Then, if we disagree, we
don't have to react by feeling
blamed or lashing out. Instead,
we can learn how to collectively repair our institutions
and communities, and do what
we can to address the wrongs
that still are present today. It
is only then that we can figure
out how we can be responsible for each other's well-being
and work to make equity and
equality a reality.

We would be less than courageous if we failed at this point
to discuss the fire-starter that
the term *white privilege* has
become. The term has become
incendiary for many white
people who feel patronized
and vilified by a group of political, educational, and financial
"elites."

The simplest definition of the
term relates to the societal
privilege that benefits white
people over non-white people
in some societies, particularly
if they are otherwise under the
same social, political, or economic circumstances.

Let's go a little deeper. We
like Cory Collins's breakdown
of white privilege in his arti-
cle, "What Is White Privilege,
Really?":

"The two-word term packs a
double whammy that inspires
pushback. 1) The word *white*
creates discomfort among
those who are not used to

being defined or described by their race. And 2) the word *privilege*, especially for poor and rural white people, sounds like a word that doesn't belong to them—like a word that suggests they have never struggled. . . . And white privilege is not the assumption that everything a white person has accomplished is unearned; most white people who have reached a high level of success worked extremely hard to get there. Instead, white privilege should be viewed as a built-in advantage, separate from one's level of income or effort. In that way, white privilege is not just the power to find what you need in a convenience store [like BAND-AIDS that match your skin color] or to move through the world without your race defining your interactions [like walking into a store without being watched]. It's not just the subconscious comfort of seeing a world that serves you as normal. It's also the power to remain silent in the face of racial inequity. It's the power to weigh the need for protest or confrontation against the discomfort or inconvenience of speaking up. It's getting to choose when and where you want to take a stand. It's knowing that you and your humanity are safe."

So . . . it is understandable that white people who grew up in poverty, with inadequate education and healthcare, recoil when they are told about their white privilege. It is understandable that people of different ethnicities and religions grew up hearing from their grandparents about discrimination they faced. Their experience is another important part of our neglected history that we would all be better off knowing. To be told you are in a privileged position when that is not anywhere close to your history or current experience is disrespectful and dishonest. To anyone who identifies with what we have written, you have the right to have your experiences acknowledged and challenge people who deny the power of classism. You have the right to be treated with dignity. Yet none of that takes away from the reality that being white keeps you safer when you fight against the institutions and systems that you think are unjust and unfair to you.

What Is Courageous Discomfort?

So how do we transform our awkwardness, our silence, our paralysis, and sometimes even our self-righteousness into action that we can be proud of?

We can do all these things by opening ourselves to *courageous discomfort*, that is, by deciding to live outside our comfort zones to develop the skills to make the world more equitable. Courageous discomfort is integral to growth; it is the first brave step to making lasting change for yourself and everyone you interact with, no matter whether that interaction is fleeting or long-lasting. Courageous discomfort means grounding our thinking and actions in the principle of dignity—the belief that everyone has the right to be recognized for their inherent worth and humanity. Courageous discomfort means recognizing that dignity is a nonnegotiable right for everyone; it cannot be earned or lost.

Of course, living with courageous discomfort isn't easy. It often means feeling frustrated, vulnerable, scared, and angry. It means confronting old patterns in how we deal with others that keep us from treating ourselves and others with dignity. When we see the world through the lens of courageous discomfort, we can see that racism is a denial of a person's dignity. We can then look beyond an individual's experience with racism to see how our institutions have been built to create an intricate web of systems to deny Black, Indigenous, and people of color their dignity. This is the systemic racism that has insidiously denied financial, educational, and social opportunities, and even liberty to so many, based on the color of their skin. Here's a way to visualize it from Robert Livingston's book, *The Conversation*:

"Think about individuals as fish and society as the stream that they inhabit and navigate day in and day out. There are forces or currents in the stream that push everything in a certain direction. We can think of racism as one of those currents. Sometimes the current is like white water, very strong and observable like mass violence against a group. At other times the current is strong but obscured, like an undercurrent that you can't see but that nevertheless pushes you downstream or pulls you under. . . . Sometimes the current gets weaker or stronger depending on the season and the location of the stream. But it's always there and the basic dynamic is always the same. It moves everything downstream toward the sea."

Living with courageous discomfort challenges us to acknowledge that we share these waters and demands that we swim against the current. With dignity as our driving principle, we believe we will have the strength to navigate these waters no matter how rough they turn out to be.

How Does This Book Work?

The concepts in this book are intended to be a starting point for engaging in conversation with us, yourself, and the people in your life. We want you to sit with your friends over a glass of wine or a cup of coffee and talk about your emotions, thoughts, and experiences connected to the questions presented here.

Stepping into difficult moments with people you don't know well may seem futile; you may think there is no way they're going to listen to you. But that's also the case with people to whom you consider yourself close. Ironically, it can be even harder to face these folks because disagreeing with "your people" can get very uncomfortable, very fast. Regardless of your relationship, these conversations are always going to be hard. But here's the thing: If you can be solid in yourself when you

interact with anyone, regardless of how well you know them, you will conduct yourself in a way that you will be proud of.

We realize this is not a small request. But know that we would not ask you to do something that we haven't done, and will continue to do, ourselves.

To that end, each chapter is broken down in the following way:

Intro Questions

Each chapter addresses one of the common, uncomfortable-but-essential questions white people have asked us about race and racism during our decades of anti-racism work. We use these questions to highlight the experiences, discussions, occasional arguments, mistakes, misunderstandings, and insights that have made it difficult for us to talk about racism with ourselves and the people around us.

Some of these questions, or how we pose them, may come across as racist or racially ignorant. Some of them fit into the category of microaggressions (see page 72), statements that are masquerading as simple questions, when they're really intended to discount the person the question is directed to. People have the right to be genuinely curious, and therefore ask questions that to them, seem well intended or even neutral. The problem is that with issues of race, sometimes the people asking the questions have no idea how they come across or the legacy of pain they unknowingly elicit.

"Being curious" is actually a pretty loaded idea, and its impact varies based on the level of privilege of the asker.

Here, we have to balance two different realities: those with more privilege, and therefore more power, often feel entitled to ask other people questions about their lives and backgrounds without fearing any consequences.

Other people, specifically people with less privilege who are part of a marginalized group, have been raised to defer to those with more privilege: they are not free to ask questions without consequence, and they also feel obligated to answer any questions asked of them. For all of these reasons, we are framing our book around these kinds of questions to show how this seemingly harmless dynamic affects all of us.

Stories

Each question will lead into a story or two that illustrates the context and meaning behind the question. Some of these stories come from our own shared experiences, but we have reached out to others to share their perspectives as well. Often, we will be talking to you with one voice, but sometimes Shanterra will take the lead and sometimes Rosalind will, in the same way as when we present together.

Principles

In each chapter, we're going to give you a principle that clearly states that chapter's message and purpose. We want you to think of these principles as the way to guide your thoughts and actions. The tactics and strategies we will give you throughout this book are all based on these principles. While we are sharing what we think are the most common situations, the reality

is that there is no way for us to give advice about every weird, awkward, frustrating, or enraging situation you can find yourself in. And that's OK, because principles give us the flexibility to handle whatever comes our way. You can think of principles like guardrails as you drive down a steep mountain road with lots of twists and turns, where sometimes you can't see what's coming around the bend. They keep you on the road, safe and steady no matter how scary that trip down the mountain is.

What's Really Going On

Here's where we break down what's really going on in the story, explain the concepts behind the issues, and describe how or why the situation escalated the way it did. There's no blame here; living life trying to blame others only stops someone from learning how to do better. You can laugh at the ridiculous or awkward things you read. Or maybe you will relate to the struggles, confusion, and conflicts depicted in the stories and wonder what you would have done in the moment.

In this section and the next, we will sometimes include ways to understand our emotions and feelings and how they are directing our reactions. Emotions and feelings are different. Emotions are activated through neurotransmitters and hormones released by the brain. Feelings are the conscious experience of emotional reactions. Basically, emotions come first, then feelings, and then your thoughts follow. What this means is all of our thoughts, even our most intellectual, "rational" ones, are motivated by our emotions. When we're trying to figure out what's really going on, understanding our emotions and feelings and developing the skills to process and manage them, as opposed to letting them take over our ability to think clearly, is essential.

A Better Approach

We're both people who don't see the point in talking about problems and then not offering possible solutions. So, this section is about our suggestions for how to handle these issues if you're confronted with them in the future. Make sure to take these for what they are: suggestions, not word-for-word scripts we want you to memorize. You have to put them in your own words to be *you*; otherwise, it'll sound like you read a book on racism and then practiced the "perfect" thing to say. That will come across as inauthentic, insecure, or even annoying. As you read this book and live your life, you'll find that there is no perfect script for every maybe racist, sort of racist, or blatantly racist situation you may possibly encounter. That's

OK. But what we will show you is you don't need to know exactly what to think and say and do all the time. You need a curious attitude, a principled approach, and skills to manage yourself and your emotions when people do things that make you want to give up or just walk away.

Meditate on It
Once you've understood the concepts and the resolutions, we will also give you thought questions to meditate on so you can consider how to incorporate this work into your everyday life.

Key Takeaways
We will end each chapter with a few concepts that we think are the most important to remember.

What's in a Label?

One of the reasons why talking about racism can be so nerve-racking is because the labels and acronyms we use to identify people's race are constantly changing. We can feel judged if we don't use the "right" word; so much so that we can get tongue-tied even trying. At the same time, how we label people's identity and knowing when and where to use these labels matters. We aren't saying this to be politically correct; we don't care about that. What we care about is giving you an understanding of these terms so you are informed and feel competent when topics of race come up.

With that as our approach, here are the terms we will use in this book and why:

Black: Generally describes a person of African or Caribbean descent. Some may prefer to identify themselves as Black and/or by the country their family comes from—like Kenyan American or Jamaican American. You probably notice that most white people use the words "African American" when describing someone who is Black, while Black people are comfortable referring to themselves as Black *or* African American. Many people in the United States consider the term "African American" the more polite choice, but this isn't always accurate; some Black people may not be American, while others may not trace their ancestry to Africa.

POC: Stands for "people of color" and is an umbrella term that refers to anyone who isn't white. It's been criticized in the past for being too broad because it groups people of many cultures together as if they are one. Because the term is so expansive, it tends to lose some of its perceived power of belonging and membership for people who aren't white, particularly when used to discuss the specific, separate struggles faced by people of color with different ethnic backgrounds.

Indigenous (as used in the United States): Describes the native inhabitants of North America. Indigenous is a broad term to recognize the people who originally occupied North American land, but more specific terms include Native Americans, First Nations, and Native Alaskans or Alaskan Natives. Like people who identify as Black, Indigenous people's forcible removal from their lands and genocide of their people (most notably the recent discoveries of mass graves of murdered Indigenous children) speaks to the importance of identifying how white institutions and the people who acted on their behalf then and continue to act today extend this painful legacy.

Latinx: Describes a person of Latin American origin or descent living in the United States. This is complicated because in Spanish, nouns are gendered (i.e., Latino for male or Latina for female). *Latinx* is a modified term to remove the gender of the word, and there are many people in this community that don't associate with the word *Latinx*. And what about the word Hispanic? Why don't we use this word anymore? The US government adopted the word Hispanic in the early 1970s as a universal term that could serve to include all Spanish-speaking groups. Now Hispanic has fallen out of favor because people from North, Central, and South America don't usually feel that this word reflects their culture.

Asian Americans and Pacific Islanders (AAPI): This is another acronym that represents an enormous group of countries, ethnicities, languages, and religions. An Asian American is a person having origins in East Asia, Southeast Asia, or South Asia. A Native Hawaiian/Pacific Islander is a person having origins in any of the original peoples of Oceania. Oceania is composed of three major island groups: Polynesia (New Zealand, Easter Island, the Hawaiian Islands, Rotuma, Midway Islands, Samoa, American Samoa, Tonga, Tuvalu, Cook Islands, and French Polynesia); Micronesia (Guam, Palau, the Mariana Islands, Wake Island, the Marshall Islands, Kiribati, Nauru, and the Federated States of Micronesia); and Melanesia (Fiji, New Caledonia, Vanuatu, Solomon Islands, West Papua, Torres Strait Islands, and New Guinea).

Obviously, the AAPI label aspires to unify a wide range of communities with common cause and shared experiences, and many feel it flattens and erases entire cultures. But like someone from Kenya who identifies as Kenyan American, people from this group can identify by their country of origin. We expect this term to change in the near future, and hopefully the change is made by people in the community.

BIPOC (pronounced bye-pock): This term is the most recent addition to the race label world, and it stands for "Black, Indigenous, and people of color." BIPOC is used more frequently now instead of people of color, for the important reason that individual groups within the "people of color" category have different histories and face different patterns of discrimination and prejudice. As we said above, because Black people were brought to this country as enslaved people and Indigenous people were forcibly removed from their land and systematically killed, the consequences of these experiences impact those communities to this day in different ways than other minority groups. And . . . while all of this is true, BIPOC is still something that doesn't easily roll off the tongue for a lot of us, including those who identify as Black, Indigenous, and people of color. And where is the "AAPI" in BIPOC for Asian Americans and Pacific Islanders? Where is the "L" in BIPOC for the Latinx community? Well, the letters aren't there, but the presence is.

Remember, labels are also about what the individual person chooses to identify as. We have talked to people who identify as Asian American or Latinx who feel included in the BIPOC term. One woman we spoke with is a Mexican immigrant to the United States; she told us she doesn't use the term BIPOC in her everyday language, but she does in her graduate school. Outside of academia she feels included in the term "people of color" because her generation, Gen X, is more closely aligned with that term. Conversely, Brenda Gonzalez Ricards, host of the *Tamarindo* podcast and a Mexican immigrant to the United States, likes the term BIPOC because it elevates the word Indigenous. For her, that elevation is important because she was taught to erase that part of her identity even though so much of her Mexican heritage connected to Native Americans. Identifying with Indigenous and intentionally using it allows her and others to claim their heritage in a way that feels good to them.

In this book we will use the acronym when we are referring to a group of people, and we will spell it out when we are referring to a specific person.

Note: You may notice throughout our book that we capitalize Black *and not* white. *The Columbia Journalism School, the Associated Press, and many media organizations do the same. We made this choice because at the present time* Black *reflects a shared sense of identity, experience, and community whereas* white *does not share the same associations.*

SO . . . WHEN DO YOU USE THESE LABELS?

When you're discussing issues in general that pertain to Black, Indigenous, and people of color, you would use BIPOC. This term is especially useful for social media because space is limited. However, you want to avoid using an overall term when you're talking to (or about) an individual or smaller groups of people. When you are speaking with a person of a different race, notice what words they use to describe themselves and then follow their lead. Of course, if you have any doubts, you can always ask the person or group of people what label they prefer—that's always a good thing! Again, this isn't about being politically correct; it is about showing that you care enough to ask people how they want to be known.

Terms You Should Know

Before we dive in, here are some words for review that usually get mixed up when we're talking about race and racism.

Prejudice means to pre-judge. It is an assumption or an opinion about someone simply based on that person's membership to a particular group. For example, people can be prejudiced against someone else of a different ethnicity, gender, or religion. Think of words ending in -*ism* or -*phobia*, like *racism*, *sexism*, *classism*, *homophobia*, and *xenophobia*.

Discrimination is the act of making unjustified distinctions between people based on the groups, classes, or other categories to which they are perceived to belong. People may be discriminated against on the basis of race, gender, age, religion, or sexual orientation, as well as other categories. For example, if a restaurant refuses to welcome or serve a family because the family is Black, Indigenous, or another people of color, the restaurant is practicing discrimination.

Racism puts those two together. Racism refers to prejudice or discrimination against individuals or groups based on beliefs about one's own racial superiority or the belief that race reflects inherent differences in attributes and capabilities. Racism can also take the form of unconscious beliefs, stereotypes, and attitudes toward racial groups in the form of implicit bias.

Any group of people can experience racial prejudice or discrimination. However, racism refers to that prejudice in addition to the socialized power structures at play. So, not everyone can experience the racism that Black people do because the power dynamic that has existed since the Atlantic Slave Trade is just not equivalent to any other racial experience in the United States.

Reverse racism is a term that is used in two ways. One is prejudice, discrimination, or antagonism directed against a person or people on the basis of their membership in a dominant or privileged racial or ethnic group. For example, this term is used when white people complain that they don't have equal access or aren't "allowed" to say certain words (like the N-word) or apply for certain jobs, or that minority students are offered admission into universities instead of them. Another way we have seen reverse racism used is as an accusation from a white person who is being told that their actions are racist. However, holding someone accountable for saying or doing something racist is not reverse racism. It is holding someone accountable for saying or doing something racist.

What if people bring up affirmative action and how those programs are an example of reverse racism? Share that affirmative action programs were put in place in order to mitigate the results of institutionalized racism (which we hope this book will help you understand more fully), and they work to establish guidelines that find qualified applicants, regardless of their socioeconomic status, race, or gender. If you want to take it a step further, you can tell them the largest group of people to benefit from affirmative action are actually white women. They'll have all kinds of "whats" and "no ways" but you can share the research from Kimberlé Crenshaw at the UCLA School of Law and Columbia Law School, where she specializes in race and gender issues. Some of her research has shown how gender was the missing puzzle piece in affirmative action that is not talked about enough. In the *The Affirmative Action Puzzle*, Melvin Urofsky writes how white women have been the greatest beneficiaries to affirmative action partly because they went to the same high schools that their brothers did or lived in neighborhoods with better schools compared to Black people, Indigenous people, and some people of color.

Now, Let's Begin.

Many years ago, we began a conversation about race that has never stopped, and now we are inviting you to join us. We will share with you our moments of vulnerability, mistakes, struggles, fears, and the wisdom we have gained throughout our decades of working to uphold the dignity of others. We will share our best thoughts on how doing this work will empower you to have the relationships you really want to have and deserve— including the relationship you have with yourself. Have faith in us, in you, and the belief that we all can do better. We believe you're reading this book with purpose. We believe you chose to open the pages to see what is here for you.

Now that you've made it through all of that, shall we begin?

HEAD
AND HEART

We all have so much going on in our heads and hearts. How do we take in what is going on in the world and make sense of it? We begin with taking the time and making the effort to understand our own thoughts and feelings. The questions in this section challenge us to look at our beliefs, the stories we tell ourselves, and our actions in new ways. Challenging ourselves doesn't always feel good. It can be ugly and frightening and over-whelming. Many of us have been conditioned to believe that we can't heal ourselves or our fami-lies, let alone our communities; that we can't be courageous. But our minds and hearts are brave. We strive for purpose; we desire connection with others and contribution to others. That's what gives our lives meaning and gives us the courage to overcome our discomfort.

Why Should I Get Involved?

STUDENT

I'm a white female college student at a predominately white, majority liberal institution on the East Coast. A professor decided to use the "great American novel" as required reading and was comfortable using all the language in the novel in her class, including a racial slur. Even reading the novel on my own made me uncomfortable but hearing the slur repeated in class just didn't feel right to me. I wanted to say something, but I also wanted to graduate and not tick off my professors in the process. I mean, would this professor punish me for disagreeing with her teaching? Would I be a target for this department as being difficult by ruffling feathers? Why should I even say anything when technically, the slur didn't have anything to do with me? I mean, the professor was using it in the context of the selected text, not to harm. But, honestly, hearing the slur made me uncomfortable. The fact that the slur took away dignity, then and now, made me sick to my stomach. I couldn't be silent, not only because of my Black peers in my class but for all Black people. I just couldn't. I decided to speak with the department chair even though I was scared to death.

Demanding that all people are treated with dignity takes courageous discomfort.

What's Really Going On

Most of us have experienced wanting to speak out against or up to a person of power in our lives and we stayed silent. We are silent for similar reasons as this student was; we are afraid to go against someone with more authority because we fear the consequences. This student didn't have anything to gain by speaking up. She potentially had a lot to lose. The professor could dismiss her complaint for being too sensitive, might not take her seriously, or give her a bad grade. And yet, she spoke up anyway. And she didn't complain about it anonymously on social media so people could attack this professor. She spoke directly to the people responsible for the students'

education. She acted because she recognized that the professor, regardless of the intent, was violating the dignity of Black people. How? By choosing that book as a text for the class without framing how racial slurs are an intrinsic strategy to dehumanize people. By not creating a protocol for how students will discuss the information. Finally, by using the racial slur in class, this professor is sending a clear message that it is OK to use racial slurs without appropriately teaching their context or acknowledging the pain they cause today. The professor decided to create an educational environment where their right to teach how they want is more important than creating a learning environment where all the students are treated with dignity. The irony is that the only way students can truly learn, especially when topics are difficult, is when every person is treated with dignity.

The book was used in an academic setting, which tends to allow more freedom of expression—even though academic settings don't exclude us from insensitive decisions. The book was written in the nineteenth century, when the N-word was a common word used to dehumanize Black people. In other words, the N-word has always been a racial slur. The book, and others like it, are recognized and celebrated as part of the fabric of American culture and as such reflect the presence of racism and legacy of slavery. As this is an academic setting, if the goal is to learn from a novel about America, then we also have to address a time in America when racism was public, common, and permissible.

It's not that this student wasn't aware of the time that the book was written or even the context in which the slur was used. She went to the department chair because she felt the dignity of her peers was violated. She felt her own dignity was violated as well. Speaking to the department chair was a display of courageous discomfort.

The chair's response to the student was that the word is in the book, and we shouldn't censor words that are in a book. We agree; censorship doesn't help anyone. But, that line of thinking misses the opportunity to truly understand not only the context of the book when it was written, as well as what it can teach us about the world we live in now. It also shows that adults can be more interested in their rights than their responsibility to teach within a present framework contrary to the content they are teaching. Should a teacher be so committed to using, without comment, the literal words of a book from another time without considering their present impact?

THINK ABOUT IT
What does living with dignity mean to you?

A Better Approach

We are all going to be in situations like this student where we ask ourselves: What is the right thing to do? We need a guiding principle to help us think through the problem and decide what's at stake. These moments feel frightening and are not always easy to navigate. This is the moment we wrote about in the introduction: when you feel like you are driving down a mountain road where you can't see around the curve. You may go a little slower and your hands may sweat while driving, but you keep driving. Not knowing what's around the curve can stop you from being courageous. But you continue driving anyway. This student didn't know what the consequences would be, she couldn't see around the curve—so her decision was based on recognizing the inherent worth of the Black students in the class, and acknowledging that the professor using the N-word in class so callously was a denial of their dignity.

When experiencing or allowing others to experience dignity is the foundation of our actions, we feel calm and centered; our hearts and minds are reassured because we know we have the courage to face situations that we want to run away from. When dignity is a foundation of our relationships, we feel recognized, acknowledged, included, and safe, and we want others to feel the same way.

That is what we all want for ourselves; it is what everyone deserves.

When we live with dignity as a guiding principle, our lives are transformed.

Meditate on It
What would you have done if you had been in the student's position?

Under what circumstances do you feel called to intervene to preserve another person's dignity?

KEY TAKEAWAYS

- Demanding that people act in ways that recognize the dignity of others often requires courageous discomfort.

- Focusing on dignity can give you the courage to act.

- Words are powerful. Educating yourself on the painful histories and present-day context that certain words have is a basic civil obligation to our community.

I'm a Good Person. How Can I Be Racist?

ROSALIND

One vodka martini, with olives and a cocktail onion if the bartender has them—that's my routine when I come back to the hotel after an evening speech. One night I came back to a hotel outside of Phoenix and sat down at the bar next to a man who was nursing a beer and watching a news program. "You work at a school?" he asked. The assistant principal had driven me back to the hotel and thanked me in the lobby right next to the bar. "I'm sorry but I overheard your conversation with the person you came in with."

He sheepishly told me that he lived outside of Dallas in a "really nice neighborhood." He had two sons who were sixteen and eighteen and he was really worried about the older one. He looked down at the bottle in front of him;

his face was filled with pain. "Could I ask for your advice? I know you're tired and I really don't want to bother you but I'm just so worried." Of course, I said yes—even though I was exhausted. I know the expression of a parent who is afraid for their child and losing their connection to them.

"I don't know what's happening to him."

His voice got quieter.

"He's a good kid. We didn't raise him to be like this."

"What's 'like this'?"

"Different from what we believe."

"What does he believe?"

"He's not racist but he says things . . ."

"That must be hard for you . . ."

"Yes, but that's not how we raised him."

"Have you talked to him about it?"

"I've tried but we get angry at each other. He just shuts down. I hate admitting this, but where we live doesn't help. There are more people openly saying things. A couple days ago, he was driving around with a confederate flag on his truck. But my wife and I didn't raise him like this. He's a good kid."

Take ownership, especially when it's hard.

What's Really Going On

When it comes to the people who are closest to us or who we most easily identify with, it's easy to take ownership when they do things that make us proud; it is much harder when they do things that make us question what we believe to be true about ourselves. But these are the moments when taking ownership matters most, even though it's often annoying, exhausting, confusing, and sometimes exceptionally painful.

All these feelings can convince us to justify, rationalize, and do all sorts of mental gymnastics to avoid facing the truth about ourselves or "our" people, especially if our actions don't correspond to our perceived personal values.

Everyone does it. It's called *cognitive dissonance*—when your beliefs and values are inconsistent with your actions (or those of your children). When it comes to racism, cognitive dissonance can manipulate our thinking to get ourselves off the hook from taking individual responsibility to uphold the dignity of others.

Through this lens, think about all the countless stories with the same plotline: a racist "incident" happens somewhere, and the community response is:

The people [who did that terrible thing] don't represent us.

This isn't who we are. We're not perfect but we're good people.

"This isn't who we are." That was the statement the dad kept repeating to me. But the truth, specifically that as a white person, this *is* often who we are, can be hard to admit. We are a group of people with a legacy of racism that continues to profoundly impact us precisely because some of us struggle so much with acknowledging it, and don't know how or want to change it. Rather than stating who we *aren't*, we need to ask ourselves "How did we get here?" and "How did I and/or my community contribute to my son turning out this way?"

And Hollywood endings don't count. You know that's when a racist incident becomes public and the media profiles a white person who came to the aid of the Black, Indigenous, and person of color who was targeted. If you're white, you say to yourself, "See, we're not all bad." But it's easy to take ownership when you're proud to align yourself with someone who you identify with. That's the moment we tend to focus on, while other, not-so-proud moments that got us to this place fade from our view.

THINK ABOUT IT
When have you taken ownership of a problem when you really didn't want to? What gave you the courage to take ownership in a way you could be proud of?

A Better Approach
Taking ownership means having an *I was taught certain things as a child by well-intentioned, well-meaning people, and they were wrong* moment.

48

Taking ownership means no longer defending racist behavior from people you love who you would describe as "good people at heart."

Taking ownership means looking at our own behavior and admitting when we wouldn't hear or see what was in front of us.

But how? It's easy to write what we just wrote above, but how exactly do you do it?

We begin by getting to the root of why we want to avoid ownership in the first place. It means we learn exactly where and why we are most uncomfortable. It means admitting to ourselves what we are feeling, knowing that feelings are real in the moment but if we take the time to face our feelings and process them, our path of action will become clearer.

In this case, this man, like the vast majority of dads, regardless of his political viewpoint, where he lives or comes from, wants to be proud of his children's character and have meaningful relationships with them. When either of those is in doubt, it's easy to feel like a failure.

Taking ownership begins with acknowledging your feelings of not wanting to face any of this in the first place. None of us is weak for admitting it. No one wakes up in the morning and says, "Today, I want to face some of my deepest, most uncomfortable feelings." The next step is to give yourself a break—meaning develop your self-compassion. The more compassionate you can be with yourself, the easier you can express compassion for others. Humans are complicated. Many of us bounce between not taking ownership and blaming others or beating ourselves up for our mistakes and failures, which only makes us more emotionally stuck.

Here are five questions this dad could ask himself to begin to take ownership of how he shows up for his son:

1. Why does taking these positions make my son feel more confident and empowered?

2. What in my family or my community is normalizing his feelings?

3. How can I strengthen my relationship with my son so that he sees that treating people with dignity is the way to be an honorable man?

4. Have I demonstrated these actions?

5. Have I asked him directly, "Have I ever given you any indication that this is how people should be treated?"

Here's the good part of all this hard work: **Taking ownership when it's hard is never about shame, it's always about growth.** Read that again. *Taking ownership when it's hard is never about shame, it's always about growth.* Growth that will directly connect to your happiness because it provides you meaning beyond yourself, strengthens your social connection with others, and offers insights you wouldn't have seen before. When we do this, we recognize our own dignity and, in this case, a dad showing his son what an honorable, resilient, emotionally strong man acts like in his closest relationships.

So, what did I tell this dad? I told the dad to go home, find a quiet time with no one else around, and say some version of the following to his son to open the door to a conversation:

I know we aren't getting along, and I love you. You're my son and I want to understand you better. I'm also worried and upset about the things you've been saying about people of other races. We don't have to do this now, but maybe in the next day or two I'd like to hear from you where your opinions are coming from and how our family values fit into those opinions. Again, you're my son, and having a relationship with you is important to me, and part of being a family is talking about the things that are hard.

Meditate on It
What is one area of your life that you would like to take ownership of to address racism?

What is the smallest act of courage you can do to take that ownership?

KEY TAKEAWAYS

- Taking ownership when it's hard is never about shaming ourselves or others. It is always about personal growth.

- Holding ourselves accountable begins with developing our self-compassion.

- If we find the courage to understand the power of cognitive dissonance to perpetuate racism, and begin to challenge it, we can realign our beliefs and actions in a way that upholds the dignity of ourselves and others.

Would It Help to Say I'm Sorry?

SHANTERRA

Getting my body moving is important to me—it's good for my physical, as well as mental, health. But after learning Ahmaud Arbery was killed by two white men while he was jogging down a residential street in Georgia, as I laced up my sneakers to go for a jog through my neighborhood, the day felt different. Ahmaud's killing made me so sad, but also really angry. I kept thinking, *It happened again.* An unarmed Black man was killed by white men, one a former police detective. When the news broke about Ahmaud's murder, the men who killed him were at home, relaxing with their families. I felt heavy with emotion and needed to move. After my run, I posted a video in my Instagram Story where I said, "Enough people are not angry, and I just wanted to do my part.

Hopefully, you get out there and move. And if you are going to move your body today, move with Ahmaud in mind."

Later on that afternoon, I received this message from an Instagram follower who I'd met once at a conference:

I haven't said as much as I should, mainly because I am a white girl who is afraid of saying it wrong. I know I have privilege. As a woman, I know I have to watch my back but I would be less likely to be gunned down in the middle of a street just because someone wanted to. And I am sorry this is the reality for my Black brothers. Julie

When I read Julie's message, my first thought wasn't "Oh that's nice" or "Thank you" or anything remotely close to that. My first thought was that she should say this to people who look like her instead of me. This was not because I didn't value Julie's words; I knew she was sincere. But, while Julie's message was sent *to* me, it really wasn't *for* me. I noticed her fear of saying it wrong and I wanted her to know she said it right. My response to her was: *Sounds like you said it perfectly to me. Keep saying just that, especially to white people. White people need to hear from white people because clearly hearing it from Black people and other people of color isn't working. At all.*

It's been so hard to receive well-meaning messages from white people. Hard because I often just don't know what to say. I usually give more superficial responses when I get messages like this. Why was I able to be more honest with Julie than I usually am with others? The only way I can explain it is I was in a place where I didn't feel like giving canned answers. I was so heartbroken over Ahmaud. He could have been anyone in my family and he was doing what I did almost every day, jogging through a neighborhood. His death didn't deserve a passive response. His death deserved the truth. When given the opportunity to talk about his death, I felt I owed him the truth.

Be prepared to bear witness and sit with others in their grief.

What's Really Going On

Every time another Black person is murdered because of racism and racial profiling, it feels like a message is sent around to white people telling them that people of color, specifically Black people, expect them to apologize. For the summer of 2020, this started after Ahmaud's murder. Then Breonna Taylor's murder. Then George Floyd's murder. We understand that some white people may feel blame, guilt, confusion, shame, or defensiveness as they bear witness to injustice and violence against Black people, Indigenous people, and people of color. But we need to talk about how people offer these messages of condolence and support.

Black, Indigenous, and people of color aren't asking for, and really don't need, an apology from white people for having privilege.

Black people don't expect white people to apologize for slavery.

Honestly, an apology isn't needed from white people for being white.

Many Black people have received messages like "thinking of you," "praying for you," or "you're on my mind" from white people after the murders of people like Atatiana Jefferson, Botham Jean, Philando Castile, and Elijah McClain. But after the murder of George Floyd in the summer of 2020 these messages intensified. But Julie's message was different because it felt like she was addressing something bigger. Her message didn't center her as a victim, and it wasn't said in a way that implied that Shanterra had to comfort her. Her message was about the overall devastating consequence of racism.

Here is a way to think about the difference: You know how when someone dies, and you take over a casserole dish but you hope a person you don't know answers the door so you can drop it off? You want to do the polite thing but the thought of being with a person in their grief seems too awkward and overwhelming? That's the "thinking of you," "praying for you," and "you're on my mind" messages.

At first glance, Julie's message could look like all the other casserole drop-offs. But it wasn't and here's why. In a few short sentences, Julie took the casserole inside and sat in the grief with the other mourners. Part of recognizing Shanterra's grief was acknowledging her white privilege that made her life so much safer. That's why Shanterra felt like she could respond more honestly to Julie and help her transform her feelings of powerlessness into action.

There is a tension between expressing the sorrow any decent person feels about the state of our society and apologizing for how you may have benefited from it. For some white people, sitting with the knowledge that "your" people are responsible for violence against Black people, Indigenous people, and other people of color and that you might share guilt by association, may add to your feelings of powerlessness. In Julie's case, saying "I'm sorry" as a declaration is way more powerful than the "thinking of you," "praying for you," and the "you're on my mind" messages.

If you're white and reading this, you could have several reasonable responses to what we just wrote. You may be thinking, *I can't apologize for the world I was born into.* Maybe you grew up in a family where racism was normal or one that wasn't overtly racist (or homophobic or sexist for that matter) but no one talked about it, and so you developed biases without an honest, safe place to process them. Maybe you just didn't know this was the way things are, and now that you do, you feel terrible but have

no practice taking action to address it. Or you may wonder why we can't focus on the things that bring people together, that we are more similar than we are different, and why focus on the bad things when we could focus instead on the positive?

Those feelings and questions all make total sense. Most of us have been conditioned to accept the worldview we were taught by the people we were raised to listen to—not just our parents and grandparents but other people in positions of authority in our lives. Most of us struggle to process and communicate negative feelings and want to avoid being in the presence of others who are in pain or angry. When we are in situations like this, we can react by refusing to face these experiences or lash out at the people we think are making us feel bad.

Now, just for a moment, put that all aside.

Imagine you're back in elementary school and every day a bully goes out of their way to make your life miserable. One day they spread lies about you. The next day they won't let you play in their game at recess. The next day they call you a name that you hate and laugh at you when you get upset. The day after that they trip you but tell the teacher that you started it and the teacher believes the bully. And every day, when the bully isn't looking, one of the bully's friends says to you, "I'm sorry." The first time they say it, you appreciate it. The second time, it's annoying. But by the third time, you are enraged. Why won't this kid do anything to stop the bully instead of just apologizing to you?

The feeling is very similar when an apology is sent to people of color. How much does an expression of sympathy matter if white people aren't willing to actively participate in challenging a culture that makes the degradation of others an everyday reality? In some ways, the *I'm sorry* actually just feeds into the problem because extending an apology creates a false sense of having taken action. It feels a lot like apologizing behind the bully's back. It doesn't change the behavior of the bully. The biggest lesson you learn about this well-meaning friend is that they can't be trusted to back you up. In fact, the only thing you can rely on is that they will continue to let you be targeted and the person in authority who is supposed to fairly enforce rules backs up the bully as well.

So, after yet another example of systemic racism's brutality, the apology to the Black person, or Indigenous person, or any person of color may not mean as much as the white person may assume. It's not personal; it's the reality of knowing the power of the system and the powerlessness of one expression of sympathy. We all must understand that when systems repeatedly, over generations, inflict pain on BIPOC and deny their experiences, it's understandable that they are hesitant to believe change has actually happened or will ever happen. This is especially true when there are other (mostly) white people who are passionately refusing to discuss these experiences, both past and present, in our schools and other public arenas. Black, Indigenous, and people of color have been on that playground for a long time.

THINK ABOUT IT
Think back throughout your life: Have you ever been on the playground? What role did you play?

A Better Approach
We begin by recognizing the shame racism may elicit for many of us that we can't quite admit. We get closer to acknowledging it when we reach out with "thinking of you," "praying for you," and "you're on my mind." We don't want to sit in grief. We tell ourselves that we'll be in the way, that our presence isn't welcome, that our presence is doing more harm than good.

Shame is an unbelievably intense set of negative emotions that makes you feel unworthy as a human being. Shame makes a person feel dread, fear, anxiety, and vulnerability. All of us will struggle with these moments at some point in our lives. When you feel overwhelmed about the bad things in the world, especially if you may in some way be benefiting from them, the easiest thing to do is turn away. Naming what shame prevents you from doing allows you to move forward in a way that you can be proud of.

In an example of an "I'm sorry" done right, President Carol E. Quillen, on behalf of the Board of Trustees of Davidson College, took ownership of the college's contribution to systemic racism. What made the apology different from a "that was then, this is now, so let's move on" statement is that the apology also acknowledged how the enslavement of Black people continued even after slavery was outlawed:

"We acknowledge, regret, and offer our deepest apology for the College's complicity, after slavery was outlawed, in perpetuating unjust laws and false ideas that systematically denied to generations of Black Americans freedom, equality, and opportunities that are a birthright. In upholding unjust laws and false ideas, the College betrayed its obligation to honor the dignity of each person and its commitment to a quest for truth."

The college could have offered a superficial apology, but President Quillen acknowledged the school's history—that many of the school's first leaders were slave owners and enslaved people built the first buildings. Moreover, Davidson was not integrated until 1962 and white students had staged mock lynchings that were memorialized in the college yearbooks. Quillen's apology was the first the school had ever publicly given.

A sincere acknowledgment of systemic racism changes people, relationships, and institutions for generations to come.

Meditate on It

What is your first response, your first feelings, when you see or hear about a racist event?

Have you ever expressed sympathy to a Black, Indigenous, or person of color about something you saw in the media or that occurred in your community? What was their response?

KEY TAKEAWAYS

- Expressing your sorrow for the latest public example of systemic racism needs to be expressed as a statement and include knowing what you are apologizing for.

- If you're white, or not the same race as the person who was targeted, expressing those feelings to your "own" people is more important than expressing those feelings to a person who is the same race as the person who was harmed.

- Letting go of shame allows people to recognize their own inherent self-worth and the inherent worth of others.

Should I See Color?

SHANTERRA

I attended a diverse high school in a suburb of Dallas, Texas. "Diverse," meaning all my teachers and administrators were white, the students were majority white, and we had some Black, Asian, and Latinx students. One of my favorite joys of high school was singing in the school choir. This was in large part due to my choir teacher—she was the best! She encouraged her students to audition for special solos and competitions. She celebrated us when we won and still celebrated us when we didn't come home with the top prize. As a first soprano, I was always encouraged by her to try for notes and songs out of my comfort zone, including opera pieces. As a Black girl, singing opera wasn't what any of my other friends at my local public high school were doing so I considered it a big deal. One day in the choir room my teacher looked at me and said, "Shanterra, when I look at you, I don't see color." I won't lie, I loved what she said. From my perspective, she didn't see my color because I blended in with everyone else. It's what every awkward fifteen-year-old Black student in a majority-white high school wants to hear: that she fits in.

At dinner, I told my mom, Esther, this great news. She, however, did not meet me in my happy place. Instead, she looked at me as if I had lost my mind. "How could your choir teacher say such a thing?" she said incredulously. Realizing she didn't actually want an answer, I listened as my mom explained to me that my teacher was putting my life in jeopardy if she didn't see my color. I stared at her with confusion and thought, *Excuse*

63

me, what? How is my life now on the line because my choir teacher doesn't see my race?

My mom reminded me that one of the perks of the ensemble was traveling throughout Texas to perform. That meant I'd occasionally be in some parts of Texas that weren't excited about a Black girl getting off the choir bus with her white friends. My mom *needed* my choir teacher to see my race so she could trust her to keep me safe.

Even though I was in choir for the rest of high school, I never said anything to my choir teacher about her comment. I didn't feel I had the right to question an adult, even after I learned how dangerous her words were for me.

When I graduated, I wanted to give her a tangible memento of our time together. I always loved Martha Holcombe's All God's Children figurines because I saw myself in her depictions of Black children. After lots of contemplation, I gave my choir teacher the Hallie figurine, who had a church hymnal on her lap and loved to sing. My mom drove me to my choir teacher's house to give her the gift. When she opened the package and saw the figurine, her eyes welled with tears. She hugged me tightly, said, "I love it," and she placed it on her mantel. After a few minutes of chatting, I went back to the car where my mom was waiting. All my mom said was, "Well?" I said, "She loved it" and it was my turn to cry. At that moment, I felt like I had said something I couldn't have said as a student. I said, *Here I am. See me.*

Strive to align good intentions with positive impact.

What's Really Going On

Shanterra's experience is a great example of how complicated having good intentions can be in combating racism. There is no doubt that Shanterra's choir teacher nurtured her love of music and celebrated her accomplishments. When she said she didn't see Shanterra's color, she thought she was showing her connection and appreciation for Shanterra.

But there was so much behind those words. First, the choir teacher said, "I don't see your skin color" as if there was something inherently wrong about having Black skin that the teacher thought was good not to see. Second, as Esther pointed out, not seeing

Shanterra's race made her blind to the context and very real consequences of Shanterra being a Black student traveling in Texas.

What if Esther took the choir teacher's words as words of endearment, and focused on the fact that her words were not *intended* to cause harm? Why did she taint a great relationship Shanterra had with another trusted adult? Esther did what a lot of Black parents do in similar situations. Because they can't be present for every ignorant, hurtful, or dangerous thing a person could do or say to their child, they focus their energy on what they can control, which is teaching their children to take care of themselves.

And parenting is often about knowing when to comfort and when to teach a hard lesson. This was one of those hard lesson times. As a mom, Esther was less interested in the choir teacher's intentions and more interested in the impact her intentions had on her child. She knew that when it comes to deciding between short-term discomfort versus lifelong knowledge, parents who want their children to develop the necessary social, emotional, and life skills will allow their children to experience short-term discomfort so they can gain lifelong knowledge.

Now, let's pull this back from Shanterra's experience and bring in statements that a lot of white people can relate to:

Everyone is equal, regardless of the color of their skin.

A person's character is more important than the color of their skin.

Have you ever heard these sentiments? On the face of it, they are both good. Racism is bad. Everyone is equal. The color of your skin is less important than who you are as a person. We are told this in TV shows and PSAs, and we said this in the book reports we wrote in elementary school. But while these well-meaning sound bites may stick in our brain, they don't inspire us to dig more deeply into what the topic is about. They trick us into thinking we *do* understand so we don't need to be curious or investigate more. Truths slip right by that we don't notice. This is why these kinds of sentiments make Black, Indigenous, and people of color feel invisible. When you're invisible, your needs do not matter—they aren't even considered.

And while our intentions are within our control, the impact—the way people perceive and understand our actions—is not. One of the reasons racism continues is because white people often believe their actions have good intentions, but don't realize or choose to ignore that the impact of these good intentions can be harmful. Living a life of dignity includes being mindful and putting effort into matching your intention and impact. When that happens, your relationships in all facets of your life get way better.

THINK ABOUT IT
What does it mean to you to see someone's color?

A Better Approach

We begin by understanding how tricky intentions can be because they give us permission to be out of alignment with how we show up in the world. Think of the common adage, "It's the thought that counts." When you give a gift to someone, that statement makes sense. You took the time and effort to give someone a token of appreciation. All good. But when it comes to our interactions with each other, *It's the thought that counts* doesn't cut it. Having good intentions is a starting place. But if your good intentions hurt someone, how good are these intentions? Not so good. Having good intentions doesn't excuse thoughtless action. We must look beyond the intention and make a thoughtful and informed assessment of the possible impact before we act.

Let's assume that it's inevitable that you will find yourself in a situation like this. What do you do if you didn't intend to hurt someone, but you did and you want to make it right?

First, check your gut reaction. It's understandable to feel defensive and say something like, *I didn't mean to say it like that*—and then expect to be forgiven. When this happens, we are asking you to pause and reflect. Acknowledge to yourself that the *impact* of your actions is more important than your *intentions*, and own that.

It's the moment to say: *I'm sorry my intentions came across to you like that.*

I'm sorry I didn't know that's how it is for you. Thank you for telling me.

But what if no matter what you do, your impact is still making the other person angry? What if you're worried that nothing you do will make a difference, so why try? First of all, *trying* matters. It's all you can do. And you can always say something such as, *This is not coming out the way I want. I'm learning to make my intentions better match the things I do. I am asking for your patience as I learn. If you feel comfortable and I've messed up, I'd really appreciate you telling me, so I'll do better.*

Meditate on It

Do you have a relationship where you feel like there is a disconnect between your intent and how your intentions are received?

Is there someone in your life who does that to you? What would you want them to know so that their intentions are more aligned with their impact on you or others?

KEY TAKEAWAYS

- Intentions are only as good as the context in which they are said and the impact with which they land.

- Seeing another person's color/race/identity means you acknowledge an essential part of them and how they experience the world.

- When your intentions are grounded in the principle of dignity, the impact of your intentions are more likely to be well received because the other person feels seen and heard.

We measure ourselves based on our intention (because we know what's going on in our head and heart) and we measure others based on their impact on us (because we can't know what's going on in their head and heart). . . . But what if we flipped our perspective?

What if we started thinking about the impact we have on others with our words and actions? And what if we started connecting with the intention behind others' actions and words?

—Carlos Piera Serra

Where Are You Really From?

Oh, you didn't sound Black on the phone. Yeah, but where are you really from? Are you here on scholarship? Where did you learn English? It's so good. Don't we need to raise money so students of color can attend? Oh, you're not a single mom? Can you make me some coffee while we wait for the director? What are you doing here? How much do you get for aid? Did you know your dad? You sure you want to take AP classes—they're really hard. You think if I lay out, I can get dark like you? You can dance, right? You hardly have an accent at all—how did you lose it? How did you become so well versed on really complicated issues?

Your hair is so interesting. Can I touch it? It can do so many things. Aren't you a bit bubbly for an Asian girl? How do you remain so calm? Oh, why are YOU reading a book on finance? I didn't realize this neighborhood was here. Who are your neighbors? Oh, you went to public school? Never would have guessed. Oh, your grandfather went to college? Oh, are you here for low-income housing? You're so articulate. How did you learn to speak so well? You're so knowledgeable. Aren't you going to show how angry you are? I mean, you're Latina. I didn't think you'd be familiar with this part of town. How do you know this area?

Recognize microaggressions and genuine interest aren't the same.

What's Really Going On

Microaggressions are like paper cuts. You may not see them, but they hurt.

For Black, Indigenous, and people of color, micro-aggressions are like a thousand small cuts. For people who don't believe systemic racism exists or people are too "sensitive," the idea of a microaggression often elicits ridicule and serves as justification that "woke" people and really anyone who is offended by them are too soft.

Can we all just take a step back and admit that it's incredibly annoying to be asked disrespectful, undermining, or clueless questions and comments on a regular basis?

And . . . can we also admit that defining a microaggression can be genuinely confusing because sometimes the reason it's a microaggression isn't the content of the words but the tone or context in which they are said? Take for example the question "Where are you from?" That question, asked with curiosity, is a totally fine question to ask. But when "Where are you *really* from?" is asked with a tone that makes it clear that they want the other person to feel unwelcome, uncomfortable, or somehow foreign, it's a manipulative declaration of power from the person asking the question. They can then deny that's what they are doing by accusing the other person of "taking it the wrong way" or "being too sensitive."

Simply stated, microaggressions subtly put Black, Indigenous, and people of color in their place and that place is below that of the person speaking, whether the person speaking realizes it or not. And again, what is so irritating is that the person doing the microaggression can always claim they didn't know that what they were doing was such a problem or is incredulous about why the person of color is angry because whatever they're complaining about is so small.

Now you may read this and think, *OK, the only reasonable solution here is to not ask any questions to anyone ever again.* But that is the opposite of what we want or what the world needs.

THINK ABOUT IT
When have you heard or experienced a microaggression?

A Better Approach

To understand the power of a microaggression, we have to begin by understanding the power of bias in how we think about and treat others. *Bias* is one of those words that doesn't do justice to how its profound influence is present in all our lives. Its most simple definition is being for or against a thing, a person, or a group compared with another. Because we all grow up influenced by our families, communities, and culture, we all learn to associate positive and negative biases toward groups of people. Whether we like it or not, know it or not, admit it or not, we all have biases we are aware of and biases we are unaware of.

Biases we know we have are called conscious or explicit biases and therefore are easier to notice and change if we want to. If we hold on to our conscious biases, then we are doing so intentionally. Unconscious or implicit biases are associations, beliefs, or attitudes toward a group that we aren't aware of. Because we don't realize we have them, it's much easier for us to get defensive and deny that they are influencing our thinking and actions when they really are. That's how we often get caught stereotyping people. We stereotype when people attribute certain qualities or characteristics to all members of a particular group. One of the ways stereotypes come out in our interactions with one another is as microaggressions.

Ideally, we'd all care about being more aware of our biases because that awareness helps us see others for who they really are instead of what we are conditioned to see, and we don't want to hurt other people. But we'd like you to consider other reasons for caring about being aware of your biases. Identifying and understanding bias and microaggressions strengthens your overall social skills. Why? Because caring about this makes you more mindful of how you show up in the world, and it increases your social skills because you're challenging yourself to do better in your social interactions. And people generally like a person who comes across as believing that other people's experiences and feelings matter.

The answer to handling these situations better is to know the difference between a curious question and a non-curious (i.e., obnoxious) question. Curious questions are just that—you want to know more about the person speaking or what they're talking about. If your bias is the reason you think "How can this person be smart and educated when they are from X place"—then stop yourself and reevaluate where your question is coming from.

Going through life with curiosity is not only the key to learning but an essential component of being happy. Being curious means you are always on a path to learning. You seek out new experiences assuming that they will make your life richer. Being curious also means you can tolerate some discomfort and uncertainty because you become used to seeking out new experiences.

We know it feels as if we're asking all of us to constantly check ourselves, which can feel counter to just *being* ourselves. But here's the thing: Systemic racism constantly makes Black, Indigenous, and people of color check themselves, doubt themselves, and monitor what they say, how they act, and how they may be perceived by others. These systems are designed so Black, Indigenous, and people of color don't get to be themselves. But if being ourselves hurts others or threatens the dignity of others, then why would we want to continue to do that? *Why is our right to be ourselves however we want more important than recognizing the responsibility we all have to treat one another with dignity?*

What if you've checked yourself and realized you made a mistake? How will you know? By the person's body language, tone, or if they say something to you that clearly indicates you have messed up. Or you get that feeling in your stomach that tells you you've done something wrong. If you do mess up, you can say something that gets across the following: *I think I just said something insensitive. That is not the way I wanted to come across. I'm really sorry if I did that.* That's all you can do. You make mistakes, you acknowledge them, and hopefully, the person recognizes your integrity and they feel comfortable enough to share their perspective and you have a great conversation.

We also find it helpful when you're talking with someone of a different race, and you're worried about saying the wrong thing, to take a step back and ask yourself:

How do I want to come across to this person?

What do I want to communicate and why?

Am I genuinely curious? Will my curiosity be conveyed by what I'm getting ready to say?

Meditate on It

What explicit bias do you think you have? Where do you think it came from?

What implicit bias do you think you have? Where do you think it came from?

How do you think your life would change if you were more mindful about how your biases influence you?

KEY TAKEAWAYS

- Asking curious questions is a natural extension of being a genuinely curious person and acknowledging someone's personhood.

- When those questions become microaggressions, they are a violation of a person's dignity.

- Don't be so afraid of saying or doing the wrong thing that you miss opportunities to engage with new people.

Why Don't People of Color Trust Me?

SHANTERRA

After a long week, I asked three friends to meet for happy hour. They all were Black. After being seated and ordering our drinks, I asked the others, "What would you say if a white person asked you, 'Why don't you trust me?'"

In unison, the three friends replied, "Because."

There wasn't any discussion. Not even a *Let me think about that.*

Just, *Because.*

ROSALIND

Can you imagine being at a happy hour with only white friends and one of them says, "What would you say if a Black person asked you, 'Why don't you trust me?'" Just hearing the question would probably put you on edge—you'd likely look around nervously to see if anyone overheard. If your other friend responded "Because," you'd almost certainly be shocked and uncomfortable that they said something like that out loud.

Even so, if you identify as white, isn't there something in Shanterra's friends' responses that doesn't feel wrong? Somewhere in our hearts, we know. We may not like it. We may not feel like we are personally responsible for this mistrust, but we know, even if only subconsciously, that it exists.

Past experiences influence present actions.

What's Really Going On

It may seem obvious that everyone's past experiences influence their actions in the present. Not just our personal experiences, but the histories and stories that have been passed down to us by our families and the groups to which we belong. These stories are always in the backs of our minds, often guiding how we interact with others and perceive their actions toward us.

We don't need to know everything about someone's private life to appreciate that sometimes our interactions with that person are not about us. That possibly what's going on between you is influenced by the history of your country's race relations. But stories like the one at the start of this chapter can easily make people feel frustrated, defensive, judged, or angry. In the moment, if you experience someone not trusting you just "because" you may think: *Why doesn't this person trust me? They don't know me. I haven't done anything wrong to them.*

You have the right to your emotions. But if you want to see past your own reactions and understand someone else more clearly, just remember everyone has a path that brought them to this moment when they are standing in front of you.

It isn't difficult for Black, Indigenous, and people of color to name specific reasons behind the "Because," but these reasons may be hard to accept. Here are some examples:

Because Black, Indigenous, and people of color know that they can "trust" systemic racism is ever present, but trusting individual white people to be anti-racist is earned over time. In every personal relationship, we spend time building trust with each other. The same goes for relationships with people of different races and identities—you can't expect to have complete trust without sharing experiences with each other. Often, a white person expects trust from a Black person, an Indigenous person, or another person of color based on what the white person believes about themselves individually, without taking into account the experiences the person has had with white people collectively. So, because a white person *believes* they should be trusted, they forget that they are asking BIPOC to trust them in a system that inherently builds distrust.

Before you say, *But wait, I know the system isn't equal. I watched the interviews of families impacted by police violence. I donated to organizations. Don't I get credit for that?* Yes. But that still doesn't mean trust has been earned. Donating to an organization is a good first step. It helps people who are on the front lines of ending systemic racism get the resources they need to do the necessary work. But when you try to use donations as proof of your anti-racism, that's not about seeking trust. It's about seeking validation.

Because whenever there is a concerted effort to address systemic racism, a powerful

movement rises up to stop it. It is as predictable as it is enraging that every time Black, Indigenous, and people of color gain momentum to address the systemic injustice and inequalities they deal with all the time, there is a concerted pushback by a powerful group of people to reinforce those systems. From our educational systems when parents refuse to let their children be educated about racism, to blocking police reform, Black, Indigenous, and people of color know they can expect this resistance to come at them with self-righteous determination and the means to back it up.

Recently there has been a focus on critical race theory, an academic theory mostly taught in law schools to examine the connection between race and the justice system. It is now being used as a tool to subvert efforts to educate children about racism in the United States. It's another in a long line of efforts to deny American Black, Indigenous, and people of color the dignity they deserve. As people who have more than four decades of working in education and parenting between us, we know that white children have the intellectual and moral capacity to learn unsanitized history that accurately reflects why our nation is in such pain today. We know that history teachers are up to the task of appropriately teaching to their expertise. If we believe we will repeat the past if we don't remember it, then we all have a moral obligation to face our past.

Because even though the first example is an easily demonstrated fact, other white people are still shocked and surprised. For example: Have you noticed that after police kill another unarmed Black person, how common it still is for the media to focus on what the person did or imply that they should have just complied with the officer's *request*? Even using the word "request" to describe the interaction between a Black person and the police is proof of our principle; the "paths" for white people and people of color are totally different. For BIPOC, history has proven that law enforcement doesn't *request*, they *order*. And there is an implied threat in that order; you obey or they get to do whatever they want to you.

Because white women and Black, Indigenous, and people of color have a painful history with each other. Emmet Till, Dick Rowland, the Scottsboro Boys, the Central Park Five (now called the Exonerated Five) . . . we could go on. All these boys and young men were accused of sexually assaulting a white woman and then either arrested and terrorized by our "justice" system or murdered by white vigilantes with the passive or direct support of law enforcement, politicians, and individual white men in positions of power—like Donald Trump's relentless attacks against the then boys accused of rape in Central Park. Even after it was proven that the boys did not commit the crime in Central Park, he never apologized for his behavior. Our history is filled with the legacy of Black boys and Black men being accused of assaulting white women and then vilified, terrorized, tortured, and killed by white men based on those accusations.

We both strongly identify as feminists, which we define as advocating for social, political, economic, and intellectual equality for all people. As feminists, we recognize the vast difference of equity when it comes to whose stories are believed between those who identify as female who are white and those who are Black, Indigenous, and people of color. We know that there is a difference in how women of different races are believed when they tell their stories. We are highlighting this pain point because as feminists, we have the obligation to be honest about this painful legacy of white women's accusations of sexual assault against Black men and critically examine it so we can do better. It is also less about individual white women and more about the systems in which we all operate. And that's just one of the tragedies about systemic racism: All of us are so immersed in these systems that we often don't even realize we are operating within them. It's the white water rapids we are all swimming in.

Because there is a campaign under the guise of election integrity to take away Black, Indigenous, and people of color's political power and voting rights. Voting for someone or initiatives that intentionally put up barriers to exercise marginalized peoples' right to vote is a direct reflection of your thoughts about those same people. Say it this way: There are many people who are very concerned about our election integrity. If that is a concern for you, by all means, work to make our voting process free and fair. But don't make it a zero-sum game where the people and laws you support are then set up to win elections. Working for fair elections means advocating equally for people who may politically disagree with you, who may not look like you, or who live in different neighborhoods than you do. Fair elections mean working just as hard for them so that they have the same access to

THINK ABOUT IT
What is one experience from your past that influences how you show up with people now?

vote as you do. If you don't, you can't expect those same people to trust you.

A Better Approach
We've touched upon how often people with good intentions can make mistakes. After reading what we've said previously, it's understandable to wonder, *Do you believe me when I say I'm trying?* or *Are you telling me what you really think?*

How to do better means seeing your actions in a much larger context.

How can you build trust?
Be honest with yourself about your motivation for wanting to be trusted. Is this about being an ally or is it about being liked? When you begin to focus on yourself rather than the situation

(*I didn't do anything wrong* or *Why is she treating me like this?*), stop, reflect, and remind yourself that this isn't about you.

Recognize that Black, Indigenous, and people of color have a different timeline for trust than what you might want, and that timeline may be really long.

Don't take it personally if Black, Indigenous, and people of color aren't responding to you in the way you would like. When you feel like you're trying, but it still doesn't seem like you're being trusted or even given the benefit of the doubt, you may get the urge to stop trying. Don't!

Be honest with yourself about the script inside your head. Sometimes we already have an idea of how we want a conversation to go. We know our line and we've mentally written the line of the other person. When the conversation or interaction doesn't go as we've planned, we may be inclined to give up. We're asking you to let go of the script.

Meditate on It

Which of the words we wrote here, if any, frustrated you the most? Why?

What spoke the most truth to you? Why?

What stories from your past influenced how you read this chapter?

KEY TAKEAWAYS

- Black, Indigenous, and people of color have learned through experience to trust that systemic racism is a constant presence in their lives.

- Trusting individual people to be anti-racist within this system is a huge request. Trust is earned over time. You can't force it.

- Let this principle allow you to open your heart to others and have patience when someone is interacting with you in a way you don't like or understand.

What If I Say Something Wrong?

SHANTERRA

Several years ago, my BFF, Talisha, invited me to join her in forming a Bible study group. What made our group different is that we purposely gathered women around the table who didn't look like one another. We wanted an ethnically diverse group because we believed that the church could play a large role in ending systemic racism, one person at a time, and that would only happen if we decreased the physical and mental distance between one another. Over time, our gatherings turned into personal friendships. We even have a group text (can you even call yourself friends if there isn't a group text? I mean, really).

After George Floyd's murder in May 2020, Bianca, an Asian American woman in our group, began our group text that day by sharing how heartbroken she was. She asked for forgiveness for getting weary and for feeling overwhelmed. She specifically addressed the three Black women in the group and apologized for what happened to George Floyd and offered to send the Black women in the group flowers or a meal. She wanted to know how to come alongside us and serve and pray. She also extended an invitation for us to join on a Zoom call so that we could encourage one another.

I stared at her message and kept thinking that I should say something, but nope, I knew it wasn't going to come out right. I was concerned that I would sound angry because I was and couldn't shake it. I wasn't ready to encourage Bianca to keep going, especially because I was still angry that a police officer was able to kneel on a man as his life left his body. My biggest worry? That the group, particularly the non-Black women, wouldn't understand my honesty. I chose to keep quiet and let the others reply if they wanted to. I just didn't trust my voice to say what would make non-Black people comfortable.

A white woman in the group was the first to reply and applauded Bianca's message. Talisha was the first Black woman to reply and told Bianca her message was sweet and thoughtful, but she was angry and heartbroken. Bianca thanked Talisha for her honesty and expressed again how she was grieving with her, with us, as Black people. Another white woman replied how she'll never understand the pain and how racism is evil, and she too was here with us.

I couldn't stay silent anymore. First, I wrote a disclaimer hoping that they would hear my heart because I love them and want to do life with them, which means I want to be a part of the good and the bad times of their lives. The moments when everything is wonderful and the moments when life bombards us with uncertainty. At the same time, I couldn't continue acting as if Bianca's text was OK. I wrote that I couldn't take one more text from a non-Black person asking how I'm doing or asking what they can do because receiving those messages is "weird as hell." I shared how I was tired of feeling like I was being coddled and patted on my head when it felt like non-Black people weren't interested in doing the heart work, the community work, the family work of ending systemic racism. I told them that it felt like they were working out their guilt. I admitted my worry that if I didn't accept their apologies and flowers, then I would seem ungrateful. I shared how this whole exchange reminded me of my lack of privilege, even in how I wanted to grieve or who I wanted to grieve with because I don't get to choose when I want to engage. I wrote, "If I don't talk when y'all want to, y'all could move on because this doesn't have to be a way of life for you, like it is for me."

In other words, flowers were the last thing I needed.

After I hit send, Talisha was the first to thank me. Bianca texted after her and was thankful that I chose to be honest with the group. She also promised to be in it for the long haul and admitted that her work wasn't done. As we were preparing for this book, I reached out to Bianca to reflect on that conversation. I must admit, at first it was uncomfortable talking about the group text from that day because I didn't want to hurt Bianca's feelings all over again. But thankfully, she was willing to share her thoughts:

I was pretty unaware of what was happening around me. I felt such grief and sadness with George Floyd being killed and I asked you, "What can I do? How can I help? Can I bring you dinner? Should I send flowers?" The things I offered were the things you offer when a family member has died. And then you told me how you really felt and I realized that I had made a huge mistake. I was embarrassed . . . and I thought, Ouch and thank you. But I had to make the mistake to get to the next baby step. I realized in my rush to not be silent, I bumbled through it and unintentionally wounded a friend I love. It was a pivotal moment where I recognized I had more work to do. You gave me the benefit of the doubt. You were so honest, and it was hurtful—but a necessary wound that pointed toward truth and greater understanding. I was living out my guilt of my silence and of my being passive when it even comes to the issues. Now I know more, but at the moment, I acted too fast and carelessly. I was worried you wouldn't want to be my friend anymore and you wouldn't trust me. I didn't have negative intent but when it was out, it was out.

While Bianca's experience reflects that of a Chinese American who did not identify as being marginalized, the following example is told through a different lens: that of a Korean American who strongly identifies as being marginalized and is not being heard by her friends.

MEGAN
I had some difficulties with my own parents and was adopted by a white couple who became emotional and supportive parents to me. For almost twenty years, my adoptive dad and I talked every day until COVID-19 really changed our relationship, and not for the reasons you may think. In March 2020, COVID-19 was hitting the news, and I was at [my adopted family's house] for a baby shower as one of two Asian people among forty plus white people, and a lot of comments were made about China and Asians.

Then, George Floyd happened, and my adopted dad started saying stuff about Black people. I just had to make it stop. It was hurtful [so I told him],

"I don't wanna hear it." He got really upset and we didn't talk for a week. I reached out to his sister to ask if anything else was going on and I learned so much about him and his upbringing. A lot of his experiences created this thin line between justifying racist beliefs and believing that having Black friends or working with Black people meant he wasn't racist. It was a lot!

I went through this whole thing with them because they've been there for me in the moments that I felt like I had failed, and out of all the people on this planet other than my husband, I felt like they got me. But then I started realizing, I am going through other things that you're not experiencing, and you don't even acknowledge that that's happening. *They couldn't acknowledge that I was going through something different because I'm not a white person.*

[After all of this] and the events of the summer of 2020, not many friends reached out. When some finally did reach out, I said, "Thank you so much, that means so much to me," because I didn't even know I needed that. But when they said, "You're so resilient and so strong," that did not help at all! They couldn't understand that my struggle is not the same as [Black people's] struggle, while acknowledging that I'm still struggling as a non-white person. They couldn't understand that I'm grieving with everybody who's been marginalized even though our experiences have not been the same.

Listening is being prepared to be changed by what you hear.

What's Really Going On

Why is it so bad to be recognized for being strong and resilient? Because any person of color knows that they're strong for putting up with systemic racism. It's not anything new, at least not to them. So when a friend says these things, it comes across as if they really don't know you—at all. Megan showed vulnerability to her friends by acknowledging how she needed them to check on her while not even knowing that was what she needed. But their responses felt like she needed to put her feelings back in a box. Her reaction wasn't familiar based on what they were used to from her, and it seemed like it made them uncomfortable.

In response, they reminded her of her strength and her resilience because they didn't know what else to say, because we're supposed to remind our friends that they're strong and can get through the hard days. All of that could be true. Or it could be that they didn't understand her at all.

Listening is one of those concepts that is easy to take for granted or assume we're all in agreement about what it means. But truly listening means we meet others with the understanding in our hearts and minds that they may share something that will change the way we see the world—regardless of how uncomfortable it may make us. It doesn't mean we have to agree with the person, but it does mean we should hold space to acknowledge the truth of their feelings and life experiences. The profound power of listening restores the dignity of others who feel dehumanized and transforms moments of misunderstanding and hurt into authentic relationships.

When Bianca used a group text to, in her words, work out her guilt about not speaking up about racism in the past, Shanterra responded with truth and compassion for herself, while also extending compassion to her friend. Instead of responding to Bianca with the canned, easy, not-all-the-way-true answer (i.e., *Thank you for your concern. This is tough.*), Shanterra shared what she really thought with Bianca and the rest of the group. This opened space for the group to reflect, while also opening the door for the two other Black women in the group so they could share their complete truth as well.

All the women were able to listen to one another. But what made it hard to get there?

For Shanterra and the other Black women in the group, there is always a battle not to come across as rude, ungrateful, or angry, especially in response to someone wanting to extend condolences about racism. Sometimes, Black women feel they need to limit their responses to an arsenal of canned answers so they don't appear unapproachable or offensive.

Shanterra admitted to being nervous about what the other women in the group would think about her when she decided to tell her whole truth. In return, Bianca reciprocated Shanterra's care. Bianca could have been so embarrassed that it could have silenced her. But instead, she accepted the feedback and didn't run away from an uncomfortable space. The conversation wasn't easy for either of them. Honestly, it wasn't easy for anyone in the group text. But they chose to have the hard conversations. They chose to step into courageous discomfort.

THINK ABOUT IT
Who needs to listen to you? Who do you need to listen to?

A Better Approach

No one wants to embarrass themselves, look ignorant, or make themselves vulnerable to others' criticism. But our wanting to avoid these feelings convinces us to stay silent, to not even try. Instead, try doing something even if it's not the perfect thing to do, say something even if it's not the perfect thing to say. Silence gives the impression of indifference or not wanting to get involved.

Bianca wounded a friend because of her carelessness and because she spoke too fast. You may be thinking, *Wouldn't it have been better for her to stay silent instead of hurting a friend?*

This is where "the work" comes in to alleviate carelessness. Bianca admitted her text in the group thread was about processing her own guilt over being silent about systemic racism. When Black, Indigenous, and people of color say "do the work," the work is about being clear and honest about the confusion, shame, or responsibility you may be carrying before offering words or gestures that may hurt the person you're speaking to.

Feeling vulnerable is hard when you are feeling emotionally exposed or embarrassed that you have made a mistake—which, remember, is the definition of feeling vulnerable. *But admitting when you feel vulnerable transforms the moment.* It allows people to be honest with you. Admitting you don't know what you did, or that you made a mistake allows the other person to believe that speaking with truth means they will be listened to . . . that you will be changed by what you hear.

Here are just a few examples of how to reframe your conversations:

In reaction to being told that you have said, posted, or done something racist when you truly had no idea what you did was racist:

DON'T SAY: *I don't have a racist bone in my body* or *I don't see color* (see page 63).

TRY SAYING: *I wasn't aware that would be offensive. That definitely was not my intent.*

In reaction to being told someone you know has said or done something racist:

DON'T SAY: *I know them. I have been friends with them for years. They're a good person.*

TRY SAYING: *I'm sorry that what they said or did was racist. I know them and care for them,* and I acknowledge that my relationship with them and your experience with them are not the same. I will commit to talking to them about what they said or did. It was wrong and again, I'm sorry.

DON'T SAY: *What can I do?*

This question puts the pressure of time and emotional investment on the Black, Indigenous, and person of color to educate the person asking this question.

TRY SAYING: *Just letting you know I see what's happening and it's sickening. I'm here to listen if you want to talk.*

DON'T SAY: *How's your soul?* (usually asked in the context of faith)

TRY SAYING: *Hey! Just letting you know I see what's*

happening and it's so painful. I'm here to listen if you want to talk.

DON'T SAY: *Why does this keep happening?* or *How does this keep happening?* We are grouping these together because they have a similar motivation and are similarly tricky.

TRY: Reaching out to someone who looks like you and brainstorming how you can be a part of the solution together.

DON'T SAY: *I'm thinking about you. Please know you don't need to respond.*

TRY SAYING: *My heart hurts seeing yet another example of racism and degradation. I know it's a small gesture, but I'm . . . (calling my representative, talking [not posting] to a family member who just posted something degrading on social media, making a donation to . . .)*

We understand there may be some confusion as to why the first response is problematic, but telling Black, Indigenous, and people of color what they can and cannot do comes across as patronizing. So we offer the suggestion above. And then you are done. You don't have to take them out to dinner. You don't have to be best friends. And please, don't send flowers! You're done . . . for right now.

Meditate on It

"We will bump into each other and unintentionally wound each other along the way. Allyship can be a very bumpy journey. There is no 'perfect' way/journey to be an ally, and that is OK. The acceptance of this imperfection moves people from being paralyzed with fear . . . to take steps forward, even baby steps."—Bianca

What feelings and thoughts does Bianca's quote bring up for you?

99

KEY TAKEAWAYS

- Listening is being prepared to be changed by what you hear.

- Admitting when you feel vulnerable is scary, but your vulnerability allows people to be honest with you.

- Listening doesn't mean we have to agree with one another.

- Authentic relationships are built by going through these horribly uncomfortable moments with one another.

If we focus on winning arguments and using our words to shut others down to show how wrong they are, we may believe that we have won. We may feel a sense of righteousness that we have defended our cause.

But the truth is, when we dominate others, we sacrifice our dignity and the dignity of the people we have convinced ourselves we have beaten—we have already lost.

Listening gives us the courage to stand strong in the storm of other peoples' emotions.

We are inviting you to listen and see what happens.

FRIENDS AND RELATIONSHIPS

It's only after we examine what's inside ourselves that we can turn to the people closest to us. Ironically, it can be harder to tell the people who are closest to us how we feel than a stranger on the street. But living a life of courageous discomfort means once we are in alignment with ourselves, we must turn to our closest relationships and demand the same alignment. What that means will be different for all of us. But no matter what, dignity is our foundation. It's our compass for how we will treat others, as well as how we will treat ourselves.

What Does Being an Ally Really Mean?

SHANTERRA

When I first began working with Rosalind, I felt safe and supported by the diversity in race, gender, and sexual orientation of the board of directors and staff of the organization she had cofounded. I trusted the work culture. Our mission was something I believed in. I respected and liked my colleagues.

But when Rosalind decided to focus on writing and speaking, we hired a new executive director, "Brad," to replace her. Not long after he joined the organization, he and I went to a fundraiser hosted by a large foundation. I was surprised to be the only Black person in the room because this was Washington, DC, a majority Black city. I hadn't realized that the foundation world was so white. I also hadn't yet mastered the art of small talk while asking for money, so needless to say, I was ready to leave not long after we arrived.

On the ride back to the office, I told Brad how uncomfortable I felt at the function. Brad's response was what no white person should say in that situation: "I know how you feel." He went on to share that because he was gay, he often felt out of place in certain environments too. I sat in the passenger seat, looked straight ahead, and thought, *Did this white man just tell me he knows how I feel as a Black woman in an all-white environment?*

Now, don't get me wrong. Safety, or specifically the lack of it, for a gay man living in the United States is, and has been, a constant concern, and the injustices that the same-gender loving and LGBTQIA+ community continues to face could fill several books. But in this particular situation, what I couldn't understand was how he was connecting an experience about race to an experience about sexual orientation. Was he actually saying to me that he lacked the same authority and power as a gay white man as I did as a Black woman? No one had to know he was gay unless he chose to disclose that information. I, on the other hand . . . Well, let's just say I have never had someone look at me and question my race, explicitly, accidentally, or otherwise.

I was silent for the rest of the car ride. When we got back to the office, I confided my feelings to Rosalind. I never once thought she wouldn't understand why I was frustrated. She apologized for his lack of empathy and promised to talk to him, and she did. She talked to him about how our lived experiences were not the same. And not only did she talk to him alone, she also organized a staff meeting about racism and the workplace to educate our colleagues so they could show up better in similar situations in the future.

This is an example of an ally in action. Rosalind used the privilege she had as the founder of the organization to create an environment where we talked about the hard stuff. She created an environment where we modeled among ourselves what we wanted to teach young people to do. That experience taught me to use and trust my voice if we were going to create a company culture we were proud of.

Validate, don't relate.

What's Really Going On

ROSALIND

When Shanterra confided in me about her experience, I felt a lot of things. First and foremost, I was upset for her. But I was also frustrated because I knew Brad was trying to connect with Shanterra, however ineffectually. I also felt dread—the dread of having to confront him, and the worry that he would be defensive when I did.

You may have read Brad's response and thought, *But he was just trying to be nice.* While it's true that his intentions may have been good, by equating his experiences with his sexual orientation with Shanterra's experience with race, he was actually diminishing Shanterra's experience as a Black woman—one who could never "pass" in professional settings the way he could.

I had a few choices for how to react: I could have done nothing; I could have tried to placate Shanterra by saying things like, *He didn't mean any harm. He was just trying to make you feel better.* But I also knew how inadequate these statements were (and are). They weren't nice or kind or affirming; they dismissed Shanterra's experience and feelings, excused Brad's behavior, and reinforced the unequal power dynamic between them.

It can be painful for a person in Shanterra's position to ask for help. It's really hard for a

Black, Indigenous, or person of color to tell a white person, even someone they trust, when they do something that is undermining. However, doing so reminds the person of privilege to use their voice, to treat the person with less privilege with dignity, to *consider* them. Asking for help is hard and often frustrating, because many BIPOC wish their white friends and colleagues just knew and did it without them having to ask.

THINK ABOUT IT
What does being an ally mean to you?

A Better Approach
People often try to relate to or make others feel better by saying, "I understand how you're feeling. I've had a similar experience. I've been there before too." These things are always said with the best intentions, but responses like these actually can have the opposite effect of what the speaker intends. They can be alienating and come across as dismissive of the other person's experience. In issues of race, a white person will never know what it is like to be Black, Indigenous, or a person of color; they can't relate. And that's OK—they can still validate. Validation is powerful because it signals acknowledgment. And acknowledgment is one of the foundations of dignity.

Being an ally should be thought of as a verb; it is more than being sympathetic, empathetic, or simply believing in equality. It's about taking those feelings a step further and doing something about it. For this reason, the word "advocate" instead of "ally" is more on point here. Being an ally is to align yourself with someone or something, like a cause. Being an advocate is to take that support and turn it into action. If calling yourself an advocate sounds awkward to you, then by all means, use the word ally. But we're asking you to include taking action in your definition of allyship.

Being an ally doesn't require you to relate to someone's experience. It means:

1. You believe the other person's experience.

2. You acknowledge that the experience is wrong.

3. You act on your belief to right that wrong.

Being an ally means you are willing to act with and for others in pursuit of ending oppression and creating equality. We know "oppression" may seem like an overwhelming word, but we use it because what we're talking about is bigger than discrimination. Oppression is heavy, it is systemic. Those who have been oppressed know what it's like to carry that weight. Being an ally means you're willing to do what it takes to end oppression and create equality. Whether that means speaking up in your family, with a group of friends, at your PTA or school board meeting, or maybe voting for candidates who support anti-racist legislation, you are actively working to support the dignity of others who have been marginalized, dismissed, or targeted for oppression.

Here are six steps you can take with you if you find yourself in a moment where you could move from sympathy to allyship:

1. Take a breath.

2. Feel your feelings.

3. Believe that whatever the person is saying is their truth right now.

4. Acknowledge their feelings and what they are experiencing.

5. If you have done something wrong, ask the other person specifically what they need from you so you can show up better for them.

6. Say or do something that affirms their dignity.

One of the seemingly confusing things about being an ally is how white people and BIPOC can support one another to end racism. We like this definition of "ally" by Holiday Phillips: "someone from a nonmarginalized group who uses their privilege to advocate for a marginalized group. They transfer the benefits of their privilege to those who lack it." What does validation look like between people of different races? Here's an example: Instead of Brad trying to relate to Shanterra by saying, "I know how you feel," Brad could have validated her by saying, "Shanterra, I can't truly understand how you feel, but I believe you and want to understand your experience more." That would have opened up the conversation; it would have been an invitation from him to hear more about what he didn't understand. The best learning happens when a person is given space to be heard.

Does that mean that allyship goes both ways? It depends. A Black person can't be an ally to a white person when it comes to race. By the definition above, a Black (marginalized) person couldn't be an ally to a white (nonmarginalized) person. A Black person can support a white person in their anti-racist work. But that isn't allyship—it's humanity.

Furthermore, a BIPOC person can be an ally to a white person with a marginalized identity, like their sexual orientation, gender expression, religion, or class. For example, Shanterra can be an ally to Brad when it comes to LGBTQIA+ injustices.

Meditate on It

Think of an experience when someone related to you rather than validated you. How did you feel in that interaction?

Now think of an experience when someone validated you. How did you feel in that interaction?

KEY TAKEAWAYS

- Being an ally is more than just being sympathetic toward those who experience discrimination.

- Being an ally is a verb—it means being willing to act with and for others in pursuit of ending oppression and creating equality.

- Seek to validate, not just relate. Allowing the other person the room to share their experience without equating it to one of your own makes them feel seen.

How Racist Does a Relative Have to Be for Me to Confront Them?

AMANDA

It's not like I thought my family stood out. My parents and brothers used the N-word all the time. With people from Mexico we used words like "sp*c" and "w*tback." In a Southern Christian family like I grew up in, you feel so controlled by your family and if you say anything, even against their racism, they are going to attack you and be defensive. I've been accused of not being a Christian anymore; that I haven't opened my heart to the Lord because I believe in protecting all people. My dad says things like, "If Black people don't like it they can get on the boat and go back home." My cousin married a Black man and got pregnant, and my grandparents said, "You're not part of the family anymore" and they have nothing to do with her children.

Growing up, I was numb to it. I met one of my best friends in college who was from Mexico and my roommate was racist to her. When my roommate would get drunk and Jill, my friend, would come into my room, my roommate would say, "No wetbacks in here." It was the first time I realized what racism was doing on a personal level.

In my 30s I remarried and I waited a long time to introduce my husband to my family. I was worried about them being Christian but it was really that they were so racist. Right after I married, I found out my dad had been having an affair and he left my mom and married a Mexican woman. Being around them was hard because he still said racist stuff—including about his wife's heritage—but I think she's brainwashed now and looks down on her family.

My mom was raised in Michigan and I know there is racism in the North but it's different. But she still didn't like that my cousin had married a Black man. She said, "Birds of a feather," meaning people of the same race should stay together.

I never said anything about it until recently. I really unleashed on my dad; everything he's said about Black people and Hispanic people. I told him, "I have a hard time loving you. I don't even want a relationship with you because you're the most bigoted, racist person I know." And his response was, "Amanda, you sure are angry. You know I don't feel that way. I mean I say things . . . But people have to take responsibility for themselves."

He won't say the N-word around me now but my brothers still do. I call out my brothers, I say, "You cannot say the N-word." And they'll get quiet. They know they can't talk that way around me. But with my brothers, I don't feel like a conversation would do any good.

Respect is earned by treating people with dignity.

What's Really Going On

For generations, we have depended on the strategy of *don't talk about money, religion, or politics* in order to keep the family peace, especially at family or holiday gatherings. When tensions escalate among people who love each other or at least are supposed to get along, it's all too easy for us to justify doing whatever we can to look like we're one big happy family and not ruin the good time.

We need to examine if this strategy is really keeping the peace. For many of us, we go out of our way to avoid bringing "it" up. Because for many of us the "it" is racism or the political positions we take in response to it. It's hiding, in plain view, with every suppressed family argument, every "joke" said over Thanksgiving dinner, or every social media post a family member makes that leaves us fuming. But the graciousness of maintaining this peace comes at a terrible price, because the true impact is not peace; the silence actually serves as compliance to a set of values we don't agree with. A silence that effectively kills our relationships more than the blowups we are desperately trying to avoid.

Have you noticed that the people with more power and status in a family are usually the ones who have the freedom to share their opinions and dominate or dismiss others with less power if they dare to openly disagree?

As social media has torn so many families apart over political differences, it is easier to avoid people in our families, or shut down when we're with them, if they don't share our views. Even if it's your favorite aunt. Or your cousin you played with as a child, and in whose wedding you were maid of honor. Your brother who you love dearly. And for some of us, Mom and Dad.

So far in this book we have given you principles based on preserving others' fundamental dignity to guide your thinking and actions to empower you. But principles can guide decisions and actions that aren't necessarily good or ethical. Families have principles that are rarely challenged because *that's the way it's always been and that's the way*
it will always be, even when these principles hurt family members, cause internal turmoil, and make some of us pay for years and years of therapy to work through that hurt. These principles maintain the status quo as a way to keep the peace, but in actuality, they are a tool to keep people silent.

Families pass down principles about racism. As with Amanda's family, if our family has principles based on dehumanizing other people, we can easily learn that this kind of thinking and behavior is normal and therefore we wouldn't think to do anything about it. We learn to stay silent; we learn to dismiss others who voice objections.

There are a few specific family principles that are often used in these situations to justify the pain and rationalize the silence:

RESPECT YOUR ELDERS. This is a principle that most of us grew up with. Respect your parents, your grandparents, your aunts, and your uncles, really any-one who has lived more life than you. But . . . and this is a big but . . . *respect* is a really complicated word. Respect's definition is "to look back at and admire someone because of their abilities, qualities, or achievements." That means respect is earned based not only on what you achieved, but how you achieved it. However, respect in our culture has come to mean recognizing a power and status difference between people and obeying the person with more respect even if they aren't treating others with dignity.

In our families, this dynamic causes a lot of pain. We are conditioned to be silent when an elder demeans someone because we don't want to be disrespectful to a person who holds a position of respect. Who among us hasn't had the experience of being with an elder who is acting in ways you fundamentally disagree with, but you feel like you can't say anything because to do so would be disrespectful? And then after that experience, we feel somehow that we have lost a degree of respect for ourselves?

It doesn't have to be like this. We can honor the role of mother, father, grandmother, grandfather, aunt, uncle, or the neighbor of your grandparents who they tell you to treat like family and still not respect the actions of the person. But here's the thing that makes this hopefully a little easier to imagine using in your own life: Showing someone respect and showing someone dignity often looks the same. You can stand in front of your brother, uncle, sister, or grandparent and treat them with dignity even if they say things that hurt your heart.

WE'RE FAMILY. YOU HAVE TO LOVE YOUR FAMILY. We can almost guarantee this principle is repeated by every head of the family as soon as the disagreement (OK, the argument) begins. This is one of those principles that sounds good, but in practice, not so much. The person repeating this principle could have several motivations: maintaining the appearance of harmony, attempting to keep people with less power and more fragility safe against people in the family who are more psychologically and physically dominating, or feeling powerless to solve the problem.

If you love the person who is asking you to keep the family peace, it feels unloving and disrespectful to them if you don't do what they ask, even if you are understandably enraged. But complying with this person's request can also feel like you are allowing the abuse of power you are experiencing to betray your own values, causing you to participate in taking away your own dignity and the dignity of whomever your family member is degrading and ridiculing. But just because you disagree with family doesn't mean you don't love family.

Conflict in families is inevitable. Defining love as "always having to agree with someone" is an unrealistic and dishonest definition of love. Disagreeing and still treating one another with dignity is a greater sign of love.

What are your family's principles? How have these principles guided your life when it comes to racism?

A Better Approach

Wouldn't it be great to have a buzzer to tell us when we have to confront our family? To let us know "OK: now. Say something, now!" For many of us, the last thing we want to do is be the one who has to speak out. And while we're at it, can this buzzer also tell us the exact words to say so that we're not excommunicated from the family for ruining family game night? But because we don't have one of these buzzers, we often wonder, *Wait, did he just say that?* or *Wait . . . was that that bad?*

Our families can cause us to sit in the place of *Maybe it's better for family peace to just agree to disagree. What's the point because I'm not going to be taken seriously anyway. Nothing I tell them changes their mind at all. Besides, I can't change anyone.* Or *If I do speak out, I become "that" person.* And we all know who *that person* is—that's the person the family labels as always taking things too seriously. It's the person in the family who always takes the bait when someone else in the family says something racist, sexist, or just mean, and then they're seen as the problem.

Or . . . we stay silent, imagining the things we want to say as we sit across the table from our cousin, uncle, or parent who seems to want to get into these conflicts with us. Maybe between our silences, we also have moments where we blow up or come across as patronizing and self-righteous. Maybe how we show up contributes to the problem, but we convince ourselves it's all about them and then we go back to being silent and resentful.

So again, what's the point? Thoughts like that lead to us staying silent because we all wonder, *Can we really change someone?* Well, if we lead with the goal of changing someone and forcing them to see our point of view, we definitely won't change anything. Instead, if we lead with accepting that we may not change them, but that we can transform ourselves to live closer to how we want to show up and do our part to end the pain and damage of racism, we may get a little braver. If we have children and we don't want them growing up in families where silence, bullying, anger, and resentment are what they know and learn to accept, we may be able to convince ourselves to learn the skills to handle these interactions better. We can, as we described in chapter one, have a little more strength and perseverance to swim against the current.

Doing all this work to understand racism is a hard enough process for yourself without even thinking about the dynamics and dysfunction that comes with family. For most of us, family is our core. It's in our families that we learn how to show affection, acceptance, frustration, and manage conflict. It is in our families that we learn to understand power dynamics, hierarchies, and the concept of respect. For better and worse, our families teach us not only how we believe we can and should interact in the world, but they are also some of our most powerful role models.

Whatever we feel about the people in our family, the relationships we have with them are meaningful. If they weren't, would you even be sweating this much about talking to them about racist things they say?

So, how racist does a relative have to be for you to confront them? A little? A lot? Remember, we don't have that buzzer. You have to decide for yourself. As you're deciding, there are a few things we'd like you to keep in mind.

Let's first talk about when it is *not* safe to confront a family member:

1. When anyone (including you) is seeking an audience to perform in front of. If anyone is telling everyone to "gather 'round" or if anyone's voice is getting louder than usual because they want to make sure other people hear the disagreement or even if they invite others into the conversation, someone is seeking an audience.

For those of us who have loud families . . . you know your family. You know the difference between the usual family volume level (your aunt that says, "I'm not yelling! You know this is the way I talk!") and when someone in the family is deliberately inviting other people into your conflict.

2. When anyone is intoxicated. You can have a glass of wine or a small martini, but otherwise you're getting into tricky territory. You want to avoid any moments of "I only said that because I was drunk." Discounting your words makes you ineffective.

3. When you're not in a good space (you're too angry or worked up) to treat the other person with dignity.

4. When you're using someone who may be with you as a prop to prove your point. For example, "See? This is my friend, and she isn't any of those things that you say." Don't do that. Don't use someone as a prop to prove your point, ever.

5. When you feel physically threatened.

Time and place are big things to consider. Always remember time and place.

If you do feel courageous, and safe enough—even if you are uncomfortable, even if you want to vomit from nervousness—then you're ready to move forward. You are ready to prepare for a conversation with your relative by asking yourself the following questions:

1. Have I done the work to give myself the best chance of regulating my emotions when things get heated?

2. Can I be present in the conversation? Not present in the way of dominating the conversation but ready to truly listen as well? You're not asking for a conversation to give an amazing, moving monologue. You also want to listen to what the other person has to say.

Now before you make a request to talk, take a moment to consider the consequences of speaking up. What's the worst that could happen if you speak up? Write it down or say it out loud. OK, you've gone there. Now, what's the *best* that could happen if you speak up? Write it down or speak it out loud. Go there, even if at the same time you're thinking, *No way.* Go there anyway because you won't know until you know.

Meditate on It

Have you shown respect to someone in your family who didn't deserve your respect? How did you feel at that moment? How do you feel now remembering that experience?

Have you been silent when someone in your family said something racist because you didn't want to be disrespectful? How would you tell that person how you feel while still treating them with dignity?

KEY TAKEAWAYS

- All families have complicated family dynamics and family conflict is inevitable.

- Remember that age and authority in the family doesn't mean the person has the right to take away someone else's dignity.

- Be honest with yourself about how keeping the peace affects you. If you're not feeling at peace, you're paying too high a price to be keeping the peace.

How Do I Confront Loved Ones Even If They Don't Want to Listen?

MICHELLE

I love my Paw-Paw very much. He is 88 years old and has always shown me love. He was always there even when my dad wasn't. He's the one who walked me down the aisle when I married my husband. And my Paw-Paw says racist things all the time. He's 88 and in his right mind so I'm not going to make excuses for him. Am I going to confront him about every racist thing he says? No, because I know if I do, he would stop speaking to me for the rest of his life and I don't want that. But it's different when he says things around my young boys. In front of them, I correct him and even tell them what Paw-Paw says isn't right. I mean, I can't change my Paw-Paw, but I can make sure I raise my sons to be anti-racist. I'm not making excuses for me either, I just don't want to lose the relationship with my Paw-Paw.

FRANK

My mom throws out things in passing knowing I'm going to bite. I talk to her because it feels like what I say to her can be the opportunity to hear from the other side. Something that humanizes the issue in some way. I am a marine and I will typically say something about why I fought for the country; for me, the voter suppression laws that are happening around this country are one of the reasons why I fought. I am watching these laws being passed to stop people of color from voting and it makes me so angry. The patriotic thing to do is to fight for the right for all people to vote.

After the January 6th attack on the Capitol, I called her and I really felt like her answers to what happened were going to show me if she was on the right or wrong side of history.

I don't want to in any way validate the things she says that I believe are wrong, but I can't say anything that would make it seem like I am calling her a racist or she shuts down. What makes this all so hard is it is so inconsistent with how she raised me. I am confronting a parent who is not living the way she taught me to live. And I am afraid of upsetting her even more and I don't want to. Sometimes it feels worthwhile being silent; even when it also doesn't feel like the right thing to do.

Speaking your truth doesn't have to be all or nothing.

What's Really Going On

We have two stories here but there's a common theme. It's *the how:* How do you confront people? In Michelle's case she is clear about why she isn't confronting her grandpa. She doesn't spend time getting on her soap box telling him about all the racist things he says. She's also clear about when she chooses to say something and that's when he says racist things around her boys. Michelle has drawn a boundary as a mom because she decided that allowing her grandpa to say racist things without her objecting normalizes racism with her boys, and that's unacceptable. She found her buzzer that helps her pick her battles with her grandfather because the relationship with him is important to her and so is the role modeling of anti-racist actions with her sons.

In a world that expects people to have self-righteous temper tantrums based on sharing their truth and condemns them when they don't, Michelle realizes speaking her truth doesn't have to be all or nothing.

And then there's Frank. We love Frank's passion for believing that everyone has a right to vote and everyone should have access to voting. We love that he ties his anti-racist work to his patriotism and military service. And . . . like with many of us, his relationship with his mother is complicated and the dynamics between them have a sneaky way of controlling how he talks to her about hard issues like race. In the last chapter we said sometimes it's easier not to say anything, but

that doesn't work all the time. Usually most of us get to a point where something makes us speak out and by that time it comes out as ultimatums. No one does well in the face of anger and judgment coming at them.

THINK ABOUT IT
What would you change about how you communicate with your family when you are frustrated or angry when these topics come up?

A Better Approach

OK, so you want to engage. You want to move from a place of judgment and indignation to action. You've made an important decision: You've decided to have a conversation with a family member who is making you angry and

127

really uncomfortable with their racist comments, jokes, ignorance, etc. You're probably wondering, *Well, what's the first step?* We think making the decision to have the conversation is the first step. Consider yourself well on your way. And now we're going to show you how to have the best chance at a productive conversation.

There are two things at play when we decide to have these conversations: the actual thing people disagree about, and the way they choose to talk to each other about the disagreement. The "how" we talk to each other is usually where things go off the rails. This is why it's important to come up with a plan. When there isn't a plan and the anger builds up, things can spiral out of control because our emotions are in control. So, what can you do? You transform your arguments into conversations by grounding your actions in civil dialogue and creating the possibility for listening and learning on both sides. All this will help to strengthen your soul and spirit, as well as your family relationships. Here are some strategies to keep in your mind and heart when getting the conversation started.

CONSIDER THE LOCATION. There are three places where these conversations usually occur: at a family gathering, on social media, and one-on-one (in person or on the phone). Is the person in a place where they can listen to anything you're saying? Or, as is often the case with families, are they in a "public" place (like on social media) where your interaction will in some way become performative, for you and for them?

REMEMBER: THERE IS NO SUCH THING AS "WINNING." No one is getting a prize, trophy, or certificate at the end of your interaction. If you ever feel like you have "won" the argument, we can assure you that you are wrong. All you have done is dominate the conversation. And even if you get the person you are arguing with to stop saying the racist thing in front of you, you haven't changed their attitude.

FOCUS ON THE PERSON, NOT JUST THE FACTS. It is completely understandable to believe that you can convince the other person to agree with you if you show them the facts and logic of your position. We would like you to consider the possibility that as factual as you may be, you may be coming across as irritating and self-righteous in these interactions. Truth: Facts don't matter as much as how you show up in this interaction. Principles will guide you all along the way. Promise.

DON'T LOOK FOR THEIR MISTAKES. Have you had the experience of the other person

As an act of self-compassion, you may need to block, mute, or unfriend a family member because of their racist, homophobic, xenophobic, sexist, or misogynistic comments and posts. It doesn't have to be forever. Just give yourself a pause to take care of yourself. After reading this book, we hope you will feel more prepared and capable to reach out to them when you're ready.

looking for the one mistake in your argument and then using that one reason to discredit everything you are saying? Or wait, have you done that? Truthfully, we all have. But if you focus on proving the other person wrong, they are just going to get defensive and shut down. That's what we all do when we feel attacked or embarassed. We need to keep in mind that there's a much bigger goal here.

HAVE REALISTIC EXPECTATIONS. One conversation is not going to change another person's deeply held opinion. If you're determined that this will be the meal or the gathering that changes your family member, let us be the first to tell you, it won't. This is a process; this is a relationship. It takes time.

Have default responses at the ready. Our favorites are:

Help me understand . . .

Tell me more . . .

This must be really important to you, and I want to under-stand why . . .

You're my (relative). I love you. I hate not getting along with you/ not being able to have conver-sations where we can exchange what we think. Can we work on this together?

USE YOUR OWN WORDS. You will find suggestions for what to say in this chapter, but in order to really make your words powerful, use our suggestions as invitations for how to get the concepts across . . . but in your own words. Otherwise, you'll run the risk of sounding inauthentic and weird—like you're repeating what you read in some book!

CONCENTRATE ON WHAT YOU CAN DO RIGHT NOW. Every step you take toward having this conversation is worthwhile. You are building your skills, and with that, your relationship.

LET GO OF DOING IT RIGHT. It's common to put a lot of pressure on yourself to say exactly the right thing or remember to include all the things you think are important in the conversation. Let go of all that! You can always go back and continue the conversation at a later date.

ALLOW FOR THE POSSIBILITY THAT THE OTHER PERSON WANTS A BETTER RELATIONSHIP WITH YOU TOO. It may not be true, but it just might be.

So, you're at the dinner table, and someone in the family makes a comment or a joke that sets you on edge . . . a situation so many of us dread. (Well, there are some of us who look forward to these moments of retribution, but many of us don't.) Your first reaction may be to look at this person with resentment and maybe a little hate. Pause. Take a deep breath. Remember, this is your family, families are complicated, and everyone's past experiences influence their interactions with people in the present (see page 80). You may have had interactions with this person in the past, and, not to dismiss those experiences, but you get to decide how you want to interact with them today. If they are sharing a racist political position, a news "fact" or opinion, you can use one of our default responses from page 130, such as, *Help me understand . . .* and then repeat what they just specifically said that was such a problem. You can follow that with *This is clearly important to you, and I would like to understand why.* Even if you disagree, you must still treat your family with dignity, and not only because they're your family but because everyone deserves to be treated with dignity. You also get to treat the community or person not in the room with dignity *by speaking up and addressing the issue.*

When they finish, ask them, *Are you interested in what I think about what you said?* If they say yes, you can now share what you think based on the strategies we have shared with you. If they say no, you can say, *If you ever change your mind, let me know.* Then you can move on to another topic.

If it really isn't the best place to have this conversation, then say, *Thanks for telling me what you think. I'd really like to talk to you more about that later.* Then later, one on one, say to them, *I really would like to talk to you. When is a good time?* Sometimes it can be tempting to see the interaction as a debate or competition you have to win when you have an audience. Honestly, why are we competing if the "prize" is being proud of yourself because you dominated another person and made them feel small? Save the bragging rights for Monopoly or Scrabble.

If they insist on continuing the conversation, you can say, *These issues are really important to both of us. If you think we can have a thoughtful conversation where people get to share ideas, listen to each other, and ask questions, that would be great. But maybe people want to talk about something else. What do you think would be best right now?* They may want the audience, but you don't. If that's the case, you get to say, *No, I'd rather wait. Let's figure out a time we can talk later.*

Preparing for the One-on-One
Once you've de-escalated the group situation and decided to move the conversation to a more intimate setting, go to a quiet place before "the talk" and just take a moment to give yourself a little bit of credit. You are probably going against old patterns—in your life and your family's. Maybe you're breaking a messed-up tradition in your family. Maybe you're facing some serious fears you have built up over decades. When you're ready, write your responses for yourself to the following questions (or as many as you can):

- What are two or three things you want to accomplish in this conversation?

- Are your goals realistic?

- What is one thing you want to hold yourself accountable for during this conversation?

- What is one thing you can do to show yourself compassion during this conversation?

- What is one thing you can do to show compassion to the other person during this conversation?

- If the other person says something to intentionally push your buttons, 1) what would those buttons be? and 2) what is your response based on treating yourself and the other person with dignity?

One-on-One Time

Now that you have your goals, try to pick a neutral place away from other family members and outside distractions. Once you are sitting across from the other person, start casually. You don't want to be fake, but you also don't want them to think that if they don't do this correctly you're done with them, even if you make that decision for your health in the future. You can even admit that you're nervous. And then name what's been so difficult for you. For example:

It's been bothering me for a while that it feels like we have a pattern where we both are saying things and neither of us is listening.

I want to admit there have been times that I haven't said anything when I really wanted to. I don't want to have that kind of relationship, especially with my [family member], who I care about.

In the past I have come across to you in ways that aren't so great. I've tried to pick a fight with you or I jumped to conclusions. I'm going to do my best to stop doing that, but that doesn't take away from the fact that people are being hurt and our community is suffering. Those are the reasons I wanted to talk to you today.

Here are a couple suggestions for handling the conversation:

Avoid exploding on them.

We get it. You have been holding on to and bottling up these feelings for a long time. They must come up somehow. But rage explosions make people in your family either fear or ridicule you. We're not saying it doesn't feel good in the moment, but no one feels good and safe being on the other side of that.

What if they say, "What are you talking about?"

You're really upset, you get up your courage to tell the other person how you feel, and their response is basically that they think you're crazy. Then you think, *Did I make this stuff up? Are they crazy? Are they messing with me?* Either way, their response immediately puts you on the defensive. Don't say, *You don't remember the last time we were together and ended up screaming at each other?* or *Let me refresh your memory . . .* (said sarcastically). Jogging their memory is fine, just leave the sarcasm out of it.

How do you stay on track? You can start with one specific instance (remember no one likes lists of what they've done wrong). Here's an example of what we mean:

You: *Last Saturday after the game we were watching, we got into a conversation about . . .*

Their response: *What about it?*

You: *What do you remember about our conversation?*

Their response: *Not much . . . I mean I said something about the players and you flipped out . . .*

And you're in the conversation! Before you do a celebration dance, this can still go sideways. Here are a few ways that commonly happens and our suggestions for how to engage with dignity.

If they say,

"I just like to tease, you know I don't mean anything by it."

You say: *There are different kinds of teasing. Teasing that makes you feel closer to each other and teasing that makes a person feel mocked. This is hard to say but the way you tease me comes across like you think what I say is naive or unimportant. The things we're talking about are meaningful to me.*

"You're so sensitive! You know I don't mean anything by it! Jeez, I can't say anything anymore!"

You say: *Well, I have the right to feel how I feel about things, just like you do. So, can we talk about this? It's really important to me for a couple of reasons: 1) you're important to me and 2) what you said about those players is hard for me and I'd really like to talk about it with you.*

What if they say,

"You're just suffering from white guilt."

This response is a strategy to make you question your motives and any actions you would take to address the impact of racism.

You say: *I didn't directly cause the problems we have, but I recognize that our community/ town/city/country is suffering because of [name specific topic that triggered this response]. I want to do my part to take responsibility for it so at least I do what I can to make it better. It's really as simple as that.*

But the hardest response may be,

"I don't want to talk about it."

Remember Frank's story from the beginning of this chapter (see page 125)? Frank loves his mom; he wants a relationship with her. And he's frustrated and angry with her. Both things are true. We know that this is a common response when people in families are talking about race. And when they say they don't want to talk about it, it feels like they're shutting you out. This is not an excuse, but people, especially in families, often have little to no practice talking about difficult things where dignity is guiding the interaction. They have a lot of practice not talking. *I don't want to talk about it* can be a way, however illogical, of trying to maintain the relationship. Frank summed it up perfectly when he later said to us, "Her inability to talk any further and my desire not to upset her keeps us both stuck."

So, what do you say back to that?

Our relationship is suffering because of the kinds of conversations we are having. I don't want to continue on this way. Will you work with me to make it better between us?

And you know what? Maybe you're just too much for that person right now or you are asking too much. Let them have a pause. It doesn't have to be all or nothing. They have to consent to this interaction. If they can't talk about it at that moment, ask them if they would be willing to reconsider talking about it at another date. Don't give up! The more you have these strategies as a life practice, the more you can effectively communicate when the opportunity presents itself.

Once you have gotten past the initial hurdles, here are a

few more strategies to keep you grounded:

TAKE THEIR INFORMATION SERIOUSLY. That doesn't mean you have to agree. It means recognizing that the information they are referring to is meaningful to them. If the person cites something they are reading, ask to read it. If they ask you to read or watch something, do it and then ask to talk to them about it later.

COMMIT TO ASKING CURIOUS QUESTIONS. Remember, asking curious questions conveys with your tone, body language, and the words you use that you are genuinely interested in knowing more about their feelings, their experiences, and how they see the world. Curious questions are an act of treating the other person with dignity because they feel seen and acknowledged.

CHECK YOURSELF WHEN YOU ASK NON-CURIOUS QUESTIONS. Conversely, non-curious questions come across in tone, body language, and the words you use as if you are dismissing or ridiculing their opinion and feelings. Non-curious questions are more like accusations that undermine the other person's dignity. If you catch yourself asking a non-curious question, pause, remember to get curious, and reframe the question by going back to your defaults: *Tell me more . . .* or *Help me understand.*

ASK A CURIOUS QUESTION IF THEY ASK A NON-CURIOUS QUESTION. If they are asking questions to undermine you, you can bring attention to it by saying, *Are you really asking me because you want to know what I think or feel? Because that's not how this is* *coming across.* Then wait for an answer. They may have to take a moment.

AFFIRM YOUR OWN DIGNITY WHEN IT IS UNDERMINED. Even with all the preparation, the other person may not be ready. By "not ready" we mean they are invested in being sarcastic and making incendiary comments. You don't have to sit there forever taking this behavior. You can always try another time. If you reach that point you can say: *This is a hard conversation to have with you, but I am doing it because our relationship matters to me. And what also matters to me is that people in our community are not being treated with dignity. I was hoping that we could listen to each other. I don't feel like my words are being taken seriously. I would like to continue this at another time because you are important to me (and this family is important to me). So, whenever you would like to continue talking, let me know.*

Then get up and leave. You're not running away. They haven't bullied you into silence. You are walking away to take care of yourself and act in a way that maintains your own dignity and self-respect—because you acted in ways that merit respect. And you can always try again.

Then what?

What is fair to expect after you've gone through all this trouble? Well, having expectations of other people often doesn't work out the way you imagined, right? In this case, you're unlikely to get a thank you (and if you do, it comes as an unexpected, wonderful gift!). But you can take a lot of pride in that you tried, and however the conversation went, you learned something from it and now you have more skills and experience to be better the next time.

It is important to reach out in some way to the person shortly after the hard conversation you had. We tend to think smaller is better here. A short text saying, "Thanks for talking to me" goes a long way. So does a text about something completely different that shows a shared interest or an appreciation of something they like. Just do something that puts a little glue in the relationship. And don't follow up with podcasts, documentaries, or articles you think would be good for them to read—*unless they ask.*

We can't stress enough how brave it is to have these conversations, especially with family. We can really struggle to like people in our families who believe, say, and do things that don't recognize the dignity of others. We can feel conflicted if we don't want to end a relationship with someone whose values are so painful to us. In an effort to preserve our most important relationships, we sacrifice honest communication.

And . . . none of us are experts at these conversations all the time. We will feel anxious, we will try, we will make mistakes and have to try again. Most of us have to start by taking baby steps, but each step, however small, is a step.

Meditate on It
Who is the person or people you've been wanting to talk to but have been too afraid to?

Why are you willing to take this step now?

What is your plan for addressing the situation?

KEY TAKEAWAYS

- It's hard enough to do this work with yourself, but it's much harder to do it with people you love who may not be ready to meet you where you are in your journey. It's understandable to finish this chapter and still think, *Yeah, I still don't think I can do this.*

- Choosing to attempt to have the conversation is a great first step. And make no mistake about it, a step forward is a step forward.

- Remember, just because you may be ready to talk, the other person may not be. It may take a few attempts for the other person to take in what you have to say. That doesn't mean you should give up. You can take your time.

I Want to Keep This Friendship, But . . .

AMANDA

I recently went on a weekend trip with people I grew up with. I met them in the hotel lobby and as soon as I saw them, they started making comments about how many Black people were there and it must be because they had recently "gotten their checks." I responded by saying, "Well, I love all people" and they told me I had "changed."

ROSALIND

When I was 11, I moved from Washington, DC, to Pittsburgh and I became friends with Clare, a girl who lived on my block. Clare's world was entirely different from mine. I loved my new friend, especially because I was struggling to make friends in my new school. One afternoon, we were walking from my house to hers when she said that she hated Black people and she was glad they stayed in their part of the city. I'm not sure if I stopped walking, but I remember the feeling of standing still and feeling my world close in on me. Until meeting her, I had never heard anyone openly be racist. In Washington, I had gone to a racially diverse elementary school, and I remember thinking of all of my Black friends back in DC. I managed to weakly say something to Clare, but she told me that I was wrong. The next day, I dropped off a book about racism on her front porch because I really thought that would change how she saw the world, but she stopped talking to me after that.

Since that moment, there have been many times in my life that I have struggled to figure out how to respond to racism, especially in my friendships. What to say, when to say it, how to say it?

Define what you require in a friendship.

What's Really Going On

Why would one of the first things Amanda's friends say be a disparaging comment about the Black people in the hotel lobby? What is the purpose? On the face of it, it's a really odd way to reconnect with old friends. But Amanda's friends' behavior is predictable. They were testing her loyalty to their shared culture and therefore their friendships. Her friends wanted to know where Amanda stood. Did Amanda agree with them about the Black people in the lobby? Would Amanda stay silent even if she didn't agree?

Then there was the accusation that Amanda had changed— with the implication that however Amanda had changed wasn't welcome. Again, this response is predictable. When you go against "your" group and question its belief systems, there will always be members of the group who see your behavior as a betrayal. And you are betraying them. You are being disloyal to the culture and identity you both share. The next predictable outcome is that Amanda is put in a position where she feels she has to choose between her past and her present, between who she was before and who she is now. And the message is clear: that who she is now and however she's changed is suspicious and wrong. The only acceptable response in Amanda's case is to go back into the fold by either outwardly agreeing or staying quiet so they can have their weekend together bonded by their shared past.

THINK ABOUT IT
Can you tell your closest
friends how you feel when
you are upset or angry
with them?

A Better Approach

Friendships usually happen
without being deliberate. You
become friends because
you grew up together, went
to school together, worked
together, or raised chil-
dren together. Sometimes
friendships surprise us; ones
that we assume are our closest
don't adapt as we grow, yet
we feel that we should remain
close. On the other hand, it's
not uncommon to realize
one day that we have built a
deep friendship with someone without even realizing it.
But no matter how long you
have known someone or how
you met, our most meaningful friendships are built when
we share our vulnerability, go
through hard times together,
or are called to stand by each
other's side when one of us is
in pain. The strongest friendships aren't sustained by only
sharing common history; they
are built and strengthened by
sometimes saying we disagree
or allowing each other to
change and see the world in
a different way.

One way to think about friendships is to get clear on what
loyalty in a friendship really
looks like. It's easy, even as
adults, to confuse being loyal
with agreeing with your friend
no matter what. But that's not
what loyalty in a friendship is.
Loyalty in a friendship is being
willing and able to have the
conversations you don't want
to have. Loyalty in a friendship is putting yourself out
there—knowing that by doing

so you are showing up for your friend authentically.

But to do that, we have to be vulnerable.

The Power of Vulnerability

Like in both Amanda's and Rosalind's cases, realizing that we feel fundamentally removed from our close friends can bring up intense feelings of vulnerability. When we feel that way, it's important to ask ourselves specifically why we feel vulnerable. Do we feel if we stand up for what we believe we may be rejected? We don't know the answer and we don't like it. Or maybe we do know the answer and the fear of being left alone or shunned silences us.

When it comes to our emotions and relationships, human beings like things to be predictable and steady.

But, of course, we don't always get that and when that happens, we feel vulnerable. Understandably, vulnerability makes us feel anxious and insecure and sometimes our brains can't tell the difference between our fear of being physically vs. emotionally threatened. It's all one big ball of terrible feelings.

Like so many things in life, the moments when we feel the most vulnerable can be the moments when we create the most meaning in our lives. Our strongest friendships allow us to share our vulnerability safely because it means that dignity is the foundation of how we relate to each other. On the other hand, when we reveal ourselves to the people closest to us and we're made to feel shame or judgment, the relationship feels unsafe. It feels like a betrayal of the relationship we thought we had.

What Can You Say?
We are going to use Amanda's situation to share some suggestions for what to say to a friend who is saying something racist. The moment "it" happens, we think you need to say something short and sweet. You don't want to get into a debate. One way to do this is to diffuse the situation with humor: *Well we're here, did you just get your check?* Another approach is to address the comment head-on: *Wow, you're starting with that?*

Later, Amanda should talk to the person she feels closest to or identifies as having the most influence in the group. She can say something like, *I want to talk to you about what you said in the lobby and it's really hard because I'm nervous about my words.*

Here are a couple suggestions for handling the conversation that follows:

If the friend says *no.*

Amanda can say, *Well I am curious about why you said it, so when you're ready let me know.* Then she can drop it because it will come back around . . . you know there's no way Amanda's friend isn't going to bring it up again (probably with a sarcastic comment or joke). At that point, Amanda can say, *I know you think this is funny. I don't. So, if you want to talk about it, let me know. If not, I'd like you to stop.*

If the friend rolls their eyes or says, *OK, here we go again where you tell me I'm a terrible person . . .*

Amanda can say: *You've been my friend for years, so I want to understand you. It was one of the first things you said to me, so clearly it was important for you to say it. When you are ready to talk about it, just let me know.*

If the friend says, *I didn't mean anything by it. It was just an observation.*

Amanda can say: *We've been friends for a long time, and it's an important friendship to me. I want our friendship to grow and that means to me that we can tell each other what we think and listen to each other. Yes, I've changed in that I think a lot about how I want to show up in the world and how I am*

with other people. We grew up in a place where we couldn't question things people said. I want to question and learn and grow.*

If the friend says, You *know I didn't mean to offend you. You're just so sensitive. I can't say anything anymore without you getting upset about it.*

Amanda can say: *This may not come out right, but you know me. I am sensitive. I do care about you and how we treat each other. Making comments about Black people getting their checks isn't treating them with dignity. I want our friendship to be based on honesty and being able to say hard things to each other. Is there any part of this we can talk about?*

Create Requirements for Sustaining Friendships

We rarely, if ever, take the time to decide what we require in friendships. And yet we all should have permission to grow and evolve and ask for what we need. It's time to do this. We want you to take a step back and think about what you require in a friendship. Not just in general but specifically. We suggest you do this without thinking about your actual friendships right now, because this exercise is not about your friends, it's all about YOU. Here are some things to consider as you're evaluating your friendship requirements:

Define your friendship must-haves and nonnegotiables

Take out a sheet of paper or make a note in your phone. Now think about the three characteristics you require in any friendship. Think of the principles, qualities, and values that you must have from people you call friends. What will you not compromise on? These are your nonnegotiables. They could be things like honesty, trust, and loyalty.

But . . . those are the things people always say, and we've already talked about how complicated loyalty can be. We want you to think deeper and get more specific. For example, what does honesty look like to you in a friendship? Because someone could be honest with you and make you feel like crap. As in *"I'm just being honest with you, you looked horrible in that dress you wore last week."* It's not awesome to have a person in your life who shames you. So what does honesty look like to you in a way that treats you with dignity in a friendship? The more specifically you can describe what that looks like to you the better. Or you can always go to these three helpful questions: Is it honest? Is it necessary? Is it kind?

And a more challenging question: Do you require that your friends treat everyone with dignity? What does that look like to you? Or, if a friend says something that you don't agree with, can you talk to them about it? If that is your requirement, what does that look like in action?

Consider, then, your nice-to haves
After you make the list of your must-haves, we want you to think about things you desire in your friendships. These are things that would be nice to have but they're not going to break your friendship if they're not there. These could be attributes like your friend is easy to travel with, they cook

a meal for you when you visit, or they march with you as an activist.

Sit with your answers and decide how to move forward
Now look back at your requirements and write down the names of your closest friends. Ask yourself: Are you getting what you require? Are you giving what you should?

Just sit with your feelings and answers to those questions. If you have friendships that don't match your requirements, you may feel vulnerable right now. You may be asking yourself, or us, *Well . . . am I supposed to just stop being friends with this person?* It depends. Remember this is a path. You are on the path. They are on a path. We're not asking you to have dramatic moments where you tell someone off who has made racist comments in front of you. We want you to consider that the process of deciding what you require in a friendship gives you and your relationships integrity. So, the last thing we want you to do is write down a few things that could happen in a friendship you've decided is not worth maintaining. Ideally, you want to create this list when you're not in a moment of conflict or crisis with a friend.

Then, if you are at a place where you want to create some space between you, how you make the decision to tell them how you feel and what you want—perhaps you want to take an extended break from the friendship—will also have integrity if you take the steps we have outlined above. This "pause" could last five minutes, five hours, five weeks, or five years. It's up to you (and by the way, these pauses can work in relationships with family members as well).

You could decide that you want to keep a friendship with someone you really disagree with. Amanda could decide that she wants to keep these childhood friends in her life. Relationships with the people with whom we disagree can be our best teachers. But let's challenge ourselves to get beyond "let's agree to disagree" and share what is in our hearts and minds.

Meditate on It
Was there anything that surprised you about your list of what you require and desire in a friendship?

Do you like who your friend is now? Why?

When you envision going forward in life with this person, what do you picture?

KEY TAKEAWAYS

- Friendships aren't all or nothing. Maybe you are really struggling because you don't want to end a friendship. Give the friendship the dignity it deserves and have at least one courageous conversation with your friend where you tell them how you feel. You owe it to yourself, your friend, and the friendship.

- When your requirements are not being met and you have done your best to share with your friend how you feel, then you can take a pause in the friendship. That pause can be for a week, a month, or at times, even years.

- Keep the door open to the possibility of a future relationship.

Friendship isn't just a word; it's a bond. It's a term not to be taken for granted or easily given. Friendship demands true loyalty, the kind where you tell each other the truth, especially when it's hard, instead of loyalty where you are silent because you don't want to make things uncomfortable. It's an agreement that through shared experiences you will learn from each other, witness each other's moments of strength and weakness, and hold each other up as you go through life's journey.

Why Am I Not Invited to Your Party?

SHANTERRA

Rosalind is invited to anything I do. Well, *almost* anything. The one place off-limits to my dear friend is my wine club, which was started by two friends as an intentional group of women of color who didn't know much about wine but wanted to learn. Both women were transplants to DC, worked in corporate America, and were looking to build a community of women. They started by inviting two women each and then those women invited someone. There wasn't a vote for membership, just an open door. But once we reached a group of twenty, we knew we had our group. We tried to keep it about wine, but it quickly grew into a sisterhood. It was and is a place of belonging, and more than fifteen years later we are a chosen family.

ROSALIND

Shanterra was invited to her wine club by our mutual friend, Tania, who is Puerto Rican. Tania is one of those people who radiates—as soon as you meet her, you want her to like you so you can be around some of that light. So, imagine my feelings when Tania invited Shanterra to this wine club and I got crickets. I assumed this was an oversight, so I shamelessly asked Shanterra if I could join too. She said no. I thought, surely, she had misheard me. "Wait, what do you mean no I can't join wine club?" I asked. Shanterra didn't even make excuses; she just flat out told me I couldn't join because I was white. I was incredulous; I couldn't believe I was being rejected because I was white. Being Jewish didn't even cut it (I know because I tried). As a white person, my first reaction was to person-alize the rejection and get all upset about being excluded. Then I realized this wine club was a big deal for Shan-terra, so I needed to under-stand, and then accept, why I wasn't invited.

Recognize BIPOC create space differently than white people. One is a refuge from having to exist in the other.

What's Really Going On

Why is Shanterra in a club that intentionally excludes some-one who wants to be a part of their group? Is Shanterra being hypocritical? If Shanterra had included Rosalind, Rosalind would have had the privilege of meeting incredible women of color; isn't it better if we celebrate our similarities and support more opportunities for people of different races to come together? How can we create communities of dignity if we support participating in groups that intentionally exclude others based on their race?

These are just a few thoughts white people may have when they hear about Shanterra's wine club or any other group that is specifically created by people of color for other Black people, Indigenous people, and people of color. It feels like exclusion to white people. We disagree. When a Black person, an Indigenous person, or another person of color chooses to be a part of these spaces, it's not a personal statement against white people; it is a personal affirmation for BIPOC. Because of systemic racism, microaggressions, and often being one or a few in majority white spaces, we need to create social, educational, and professional spaces that are sanctuaries from the dominant institutions that have traditionally reinforced and currently reinforce racism.

Let's say this another way: Have you ever had to wear a pair of pants that were too tight? As a Black person, a person of color, or an Indigenous person, being at school or work all day surrounded by white people feels like having to hold your stomach in. You may look good, but it's uncomfortable. Or as Shanterra likes to say, it's like taking off a bra as soon as you walk through your front door after a long day. You exhale!

For people of color in majority-white spaces, this is rarely the case. Exhaling is rare, especially because you're so focused on performing exceptionally as a representation of your entire race. BIPOC often lack spaces to feel belonging and membership, inclusion, safety, humanity, and dignity. Spaces like Shanterra's wine club and other clubs or social groups, faith communities, and organizations enable them to recharge and refuel their emotional energy so they can go back to thriving in majority white environments. Megan Yoo Schneider, an American with Korean heritage who is an engineer and an adjunct professor at Chapman University, says, "Creating those spaces isn't exclusive of white people. It's actually enabling people of color to access the upper parts of their brains and experience psychological safety, so that benefits the entire organization, community, or society as a whole. Our brains aren't

THINK ABOUT IT
Have you ever felt excluded from a group of people? What did you feel when you realized you weren't included?

operating in fight-or-flight mode so we can be more creative and innovative."

A Better Approach
There are two ways a white person will experience the "Do I belong?" problem. One is similar to Rosalind's—when you aren't invited but don't understand why. In Rosalind's case, even though her first impulse was to feel hurt and excluded, she took a step back to reflect. She realized that her non-invitation had nothing to do with her and everything to do with these women needing space to be together. While her feelings are understandable because she felt excluded, this was a moment to appreciate that her exclusion had nothing to do with her. Her emotional truth was not as important, in this case, as these women's need to have the time and space to be together.

But what happens when you find yourself invited, but then sense that your presence creates awkwardness?

As we've said before, Black, Indigenous, and people of color are more familiar with "white" spaces than white people are familiar with spaces created by Black, Indigenous, and people of color because BIPOC are taught to assimilate into white spaces as a survival skill. But when a white person is added to a space created as a safe space for Black, Indigenous, and people of color, the space changes.

Years ago, Shanterra invited her friend Brooklyn, who is white, to participate in a conference she hosted called the Marvelous Girls' Summit. This conference brought sixth- through ninth-grade girls together from different backgrounds, in partnership with Sisters Supporting Sisters, a group of Southern Methodist University women of color who provide support to one another on their predominantly white campus.

Brooklyn and Shanterra agreed to meet Sisters Supporting Sisters in the student center to review the assignments for the day. But here's where things got complicated. Brooklyn arrived first, before Shanterra could break the ice and make introductions, and Shanterra forgot to inform the women that Brooklyn would be joining them ahead of time. Brooklyn shared her memories of that experience:

I didn't experience discomfort until I realized I was changing the dynamic of the group and what would be said. I think if this was a group of people coming together who had never met each other, it would have been very different than a white woman entering a room with Black women who had established a community. I thought, What do I do? Was leaving rude? Was leaving right? Was acknowledging race important? Should I ask if my presence was changing the dynamic of this group? [Should I ask] Is there a time you want to spend without me here? *There were a million thoughts running through my head . . . so I just ate my burrito. I felt welcomed but uninvited.*

Brooklyn handled this situation as best as she could—she was self-aware enough to realize that her presence was impacting the students' sense of sanctuary, and most importantly, she did not take this discomfort personally. Shanterra also could have done better. She forgot that she needed to be there to give credibility to Brooklyn as a white woman entering the space. Because of this, Brook-lyn's arrival was jarring rather than pleasant.

The takeaway here is that the moment a white person enters a space intended for Black, Indigenous, and people of color, it changes from being about the BIPOC who created and needed the space to focus on the white person: why they are there, should they be there, how can we change our behaviors to make them comfortable.

If you ever find yourself in a situation like Brooklyn's, you can say, "You probably want to chat or catch up. I'll come back when we're ready to begin."

Even if they tell you to stay, you should leave anyway because you now understand they may only be telling you that to make you comfortable. As an ally, your comfort is not your concern. Their comfort is.

Meditate on It

Have you ever been connected to a group that is a sanctuary or refuge for you? What connects you to each other?

When you sense that you are changing the feeling of a room, what do you do?

KEY TAKEAWAYS

- Remember that the reason Black, Indigenous, and people of color need space is not comparable to white people creating space. The latter is intended to exclude others; the former is a refuge from having to exist in the other.

- Spaces created by BIPOC enable them to recharge and refuel so they can take care of their emotional wellness and go back and thrive in majority-white environments.

- Psychological safety for everyone benefits the entire organization, entire community, and society as a whole.

PRINCIPLE IN ACTION

The reasons BIPOC create space for each other isn't comparable to white people's reasons. One is a refuge from having to exist in the other; *most spaces are white spaces.* Here are a couple examples:

HIGHER EDUCATION
Before the Civil Rights movement, Historically Black Colleges and Universities (HBCUs) offered Black Americans one of their *only* routes to a college degree. These institutions helped Black Americans pursue professional careers, earn graduate degrees, build essential professional networks, and advance their education in an inclusive environment, both during and after a time when they were excluded from all-white institutions of higher learning.

POLITICAL REPRESENTATION
If we pay attention to who historically participated in US politics of any kind, one would think that power and position is only for white men; just look at our first forty-three US presidents. But, since the United States isn't made up of only white people, Black, Indigenous and people of color needed to create space in voting bodies, particularly in Congress, in order to ensure there is fair and equal representation for the people impacted by policies and procedures created by our government; and that the issues important to BIPOC are fairly and equally represented and addressed. This is why the Congressional Hispanic Caucus exists. The Congressional Hispanic Caucus (CHC) was organized in 1976. The Caucus was originally formed to serve as a legislative organization through which legislative action, as well as executive and judicial actions, could be monitored to

ensure the needs of Hispanic people were being met. According to documents from the CHC, the founders of the CHC stated that their mission was "to develop programs . . . to increase opportunities for Hispanics to participate in and contribute to the American political system" and to "reverse the national pattern of neglect, exclusion and indifference suffered for decades by Spanish-speaking citizens of the U.S."

Now that you know, you are prepared: prepared to do something differently, prepared to listen differently, prepared to hold space differently.

Why Does Allyship Have to Be So Serious?

ROSALIND

I am the mother of two young men who the world identifies as white. They don't entirely agree with that because I'm Jewish and their father is Spanish (they call themselves "Anglohispajews"), but they also see why people would identify them as white, and they recognize the privilege they have because of it. As they have grown into young men, they experience their race more complexly because of the strong simultaneous presence of their ethnic identities. Both of them believe one of my more irritating qualities is that I have passionate opinions about their political participation. But during the summer of 2020, I got more heated. I felt strongly that they should be more involved in the racial justice movement that was sweeping the country.

Now that I look back on that time, I realize I was taking my issues out on them—because I felt guilty that I hadn't done enough. I did self-reflect on this a bit at the time, but it didn't stop me from channeling my feelings into nagging them, which of course they didn't appreciate. They felt certain that they advocated in ways that were meaningful to them, which I didn't see or appreciate enough.

They had fair points.

So, I was a little surprised when my older son told me he was going to a protest to seek justice for Elijah McClain's murder. McClain was killed by Aurora, Colorado, police in August 2019, although the police's body camera footage wasn't released until months later, in 2020.

My son, also named Elijah, returned from the protest after I had gone to bed. The next morning, he told me about the experience and then asked me, "Am I allowed, as a white person, to dance at a protest?"

He had gone to the protest with a white friend who got really angry because Elijah joined a street dance party after a truck showed up with large speakers at the conclusion of the speeches. His friend thought because they were white, they shouldn't dance because doing so was disrespectful and took away from the seriousness of why they were there. Elijah thought joining the dance party showed solidarity (and he loves to dance). In his mind, *we marched together and now we dance together.*

Elijah circled around various questions at breakfast:

Why does a protest always have to be serious?

Do white people who go to protests always have to be so serious?

Realize our ways may be different. Extend grace to each other along the way.

What's Really Going On

Elijah went to the protest with a white friend, and they were there all day and into the evening. At around 10 p.m., a truck with large speakers showed up and started a dance party, and Elijah began to dance with the other protesters. His friend noted that dancing felt disrespectful and took away from the seriousness of why they were there because they were white. Elijah felt joining the dance party showed solidarity because all the protestors were dancing together.

Elijah and his friend can both be right. Here's how we see it: If Elijah and his friend had just shown up for the dance without participating in the protest, it would have been inappropriate to join. Traditionally, in the Black community, grieving at a funeral is followed by the repast, a gathering after the funeral where people come together to eat delicious food and celebrate life. Anyone skipping the funeral because they don't want to experience the grief but showing up at the repast would be totally judged and not welcome. Protests often follow a similar sequence of events: coming together to grieve, bear witness, and demand justice first—only after that work has been done does the celebration begin. Being an ally isn't just about showing up for the party.

However, it's understandable for people in these situations

to get annoyed at each other for not being "woke enough" or on the other hand "too woke."

Yes, we are going to wade into the "woke" waters, because we can't be distracted and manipulated by people who want to deny the intention, meaning, and history of what that word represents. Plus, the more we focus on blaming and being mad at each other when someone doesn't behave in the "right" way, the more power we give to people who want to uphold systemic racism. By all means, you are entitled to be frustrated with someone who appears to police other people's words and actions. Even if the person has a good point, they can often come across as self-righteous or intolerant. But realize that if you label and disparage their comments as "woke" due to their delivery or because their way is different from yours, you are discrediting their efforts and contributing to dismissing the importance of the overall issue.

Where does the term *woke* come from? Black American folk singer-songwriter Huddie Ledbetter, a.k.a. Lead Belly, gives us a look at its likely origins when he urges people to "stay woke" in an afterpiece remark on a 1938 song recording. The recording, called "Scottsboro Boys," tells the story of nine Black teenagers accused of raping two white women. The term was used in a spoken word piece at the end of the song: "I advise everybody, be a little careful when they go along through there—best stay woke, keep their eyes open." The young men did not receive a fair trial, and even though there was no physical evidence to suggest they had committed the crime, all of them were convicted, and eight of the nine were sentenced to death. So, you can see why "stay woke" was a serious warning to Black people to stay ever vigilant for their physical safety. From there, the term evolved to describe general racial awareness. During the more recent protests against police brutality, the term has expanded to include awareness of social justice issues in general. But like most things, it has also become a degrading term used to demean people who openly advocate for social justice and to dilute and dismiss the importance of those issues. Some use the term to bully others, with hopes of embarrassing and silencing someone for speaking out against injustice, especially if they haven't publicly spoken out before. Or, conversely, it is a way for corporations to market to young people to prove they're cool enough for them to buy their products, which never ever works. Young people see right through ploys that aren't genuine.

THINK ABOUT IT
What do you need to take less seriously about yourself? What issue do you need to take more seriously?

A Better Approach

The work of being anti-racist, the choice to identify as an ally, isn't a costume and isn't one size fits all. However you choose to express your advocacy and support, if you're serious and committed to the issues, developing multi-faceted real relationships with people where you can be yourself, including laughing or dancing in this case, is just who you are. However, it's understandable for people in these situations to get annoyed at each other for not behaving in the "right" way. For not being "woke enough" or on the other hand being "too woke."

The history of "wokeness" needs to be given the proper respect it is due. This also means that trying on something or performing allyship is not the answer to changing systemic racism, even if you have the best intentions (intent does not equal impact, as on page 65). We ask you to extend grace to yourself and others. That means knowing you and others will make mistakes, and you need to work together to do what you can to make fewer of them. It means holding yourself accountable to learn what you don't know, to listen to the answers to the hard questions and critiques so you can grow better. Showing grace is about extending patience to yourself and others as you listen, learn, and grow, oftentimes not in that order.

What do you do when wokeness is used as a weapon to dismiss the pain and suffering of the BIPOC community?
When people, especially people in positions of public power like politicians and people in the media, accuse

someone or something of being woke in a negative way, then it's the time to dig deeper and educate yourself about what they are dismissing so eagerly. Is it to cover up something they don't want you to pay attention to? Is it a tactic intended to dismiss the merits of whatever issue they're talking about?

This may happen in your personal life. If you notice a friend using the word "woke" to dismiss issues about race, you could say something like:

Hey, I want to pause you for a moment. I get that this person is annoying you, but can we stop using "woke" to put someone down? It's too easy to dismiss the person who is annoying you along with the bigger issues. And then make room for your friend to respond. Your friend might blow you off and not feel the same way you do. Here's your chance to give them space to think about it, even if you're not on the same page.

What if your friend is super-woke and you're getting annoyed with them because they're constantly judging you?
It's annoying when you have a friend who is constantly judgmental. If the friend is being judgmental about your apparent lack of concern about race and racism, that can be especially hard. You can be tempted to blow the person off or gradually give up on the friendship because your friend can make you feel like you're a lost cause. You could avoid them because you worry that you're going to say or do something wrong and then you'll get a lecture about how disappointed they are or how ignorant or hopeless you are. We get it.

But if keeping this friend-ship is important to you, the next time a situation like this happens, try saying something like:

I know these issues are really important. I really appreciate you bringing them to my atten-tion. But I also want to tell you that it feels like you're judging me a lot or expecting me to mess up and that's a hard way to have a friendship. It feels like I can't talk about anything else with you.

If you want to take a pause in the friendship, you can do that too. Just don't disappear. You can say one more thing before you take your pause, such as:

I know we've already dis-cussed how I feel you're judg-ing me, and at the same time, I know these issues are really important. But I feel like you're monitoring the things I say so I can't be myself around you. I'm going to take a break from our friendship and give myself some space to think about all of this.

What if your friend is super-woke and you want to complain to other people about them?
It's completely understand-able to want to talk about a friend with whom you're irritated. However, you have to check yourself first and admit if you're venting or just talking behind their back. You vent when you need to process negative emo-tions and feelings. You vent when you need to seek out advice from another person about a difficult situation. On the other hand, talking behind someone's back not only undermines the person you're talking about, but also their opinions, thoughts, and

feelings (and it doesn't make you look so great either).

It's particularly important to look at your motivations here because it's too easy for these kinds of complaints to undermine the focus of combating racism. The messenger may be annoying, but that doesn't mean the message they are trying to convey isn't important—it's probably true that at least some of the things they're bringing to your attention merit reflection. That doesn't mean you have to completely agree, but it does mean it is worthwhile to pause and reflect on why this person is so irritating to you.

What if you're the super-woke one?
The principle for this chapter is that showing grace means giving people a break. This can be really hard when your eyes have been opened to things that maybe you weren't aware of until recently. This knowledge of systemic racism is painful, and you want everyone to be on board with you so that all people can be treated with dignity, regardless of the color of their skin. We get that. You can still do that while remembering that this work is a journey, not a quick ride for anyone.

Extending grace doesn't mean you care less, nor does it mean you're not holding people accountable. It doesn't even mean you're taking your foot off the gas of ending systemic racism. It means you're meeting people where they are and inviting them to join you on the journey. It also means paying attention to your friends to see what part of this work may resonate with them the most. You want people around you to want to be a part of the change because it's the right thing to do, not because you've bullied them into joining you.

For example, if you know a friend loves to shop at a certain store and you know that store or brand has done a lot to help end systemic racism, you could point that out to your friend. You could say something such as, *I know you love to shop at Target. Did you know that they have invested so many dollars to help educate people on how to be advocates for ending racism? They have really cute stuff, but I like that they're also making a difference in other ways.*

Saying this is not to make your friend feel out of touch or less aware of the issues, but it can help your friend see that you're still interested in the things that interest them while also pointing out how a brand they love is being a part of systemic change. And by default, they are too.

Making this connection may seem small in the big scheme of things, but it may well make a difference. This type of change lasts longer because they're not bullied into caring. We're just saying you may get more partners in the journey with patience and grace than judgment and force.

What if you're more woke than your BIPOC friends?

Your lived experience as a white person will not ever make you know more about what it means to be a person of color. You may have read *Roots* by Alex Haley from cover to cover and also watched the original miniseries from 1977. You may have marched at a Dakota Access Pipeline protest in your community. As a child growing up, you may have even had a best friend who was Black or another person of color. All this is great, truly. But none of these moments give you the lived experience of knowing what it means to live the life of a Black person, an Indigenous person, or another person of color. It's possible that you don't really know what that person thinks because they aren't telling you everything. So, all this is to say: Be careful about making assumptions. If you feel like you've done the work and have educated yourself on these important issues, then this is a great opportunity to be outspoken with people who look like you. If you believe you understand the inequality in our society better than some of your friends, use that information to educate others who look like you. Plus, every time you do that, you do your part to take the weight off people of color in educating white people.

Meditate on It

Who helps hold you accountable when you take yourself too seriously?

Who helps hold you accountable when you aren't taking issues seriously?

KEY TAKEAWAYS

- The history of the word *woke* is directly tied to Black Americans' vigilance to protect their physical safety.

- Don't let other people manipulate that word to trivialize the pain and suffering of Black people's past and present experience in this country.

- Don't be afraid to be yourself in your anti-racist work, but read the room. As with Brooklyn in the last chapter, sometimes the intention of a space indicates that allies need to take on a different role than BIPOC people in the same space.

We can disagree and still love each other unless your disagreement is rooted in my oppression and denial of my humanity and right to exist.

—Robert Jones Jr.

BE EASY ON PEOPLE, HARD ON IDEAS.

SHANTERRA

"A word that I can't stand is equality. *That word just rubs me the wrong way." A white woman who works with young people at a church said this to me during a phone conversation.*

Her response made me think of a principle Charlie Kuhn, Rosalind's co-founder at Cultures of Dignity, came up with: Be easy on people, hard on ideas. Even though she and I aren't friends, we do have a relationship, so hearing her express her disdain for the word equality *made me pause. I told her that unfortunately, many of our country's policies, laws, and systems are designed to make sure there isn't equality, but I didn't want to press the conversation. It wasn't the time to go deeper, and I knew I'd have another opportunity to talk to her. I hope I can learn why the word makes her feel such disdain, because as a Black woman, being treated with equality is vital to my existence.*

"Easy on people, hard on ideas" in many ways makes a lot of sense. We live in a culture that is the opposite; we're hard on people and easy on ideas. We are so busy blaming, pathologizing, ridiculing, and thinking the worst of people that we can't pay attention to the problems behind the people, let alone come up with creative solutions to solve these problems.

But when we relate this principle to racism it gets a lot harder. When I think about racism and people who hate me simply because of the color of my skin or deny my people's experience, I have a real hard time with something that sounds like it's giving racists a break. Like I should focus instead on the humanity of racists, even though they are denying my humanity and that denial contributes to systemic racism.

But "easy on people, hard on ideas" isn't suggesting this at all. It isn't asking me or other BIPOC to give racists a break. It means I still get to challenge racist thinking and policies that are oppressive, while also being able to see why people still want those policies in place. I can see their "why," see how it benefits them, even see their fear of systems changing. I have sympathy for them even though they want to keep me and those who look like me from equality, from getting ahead.

White people I have a relationship with may not always understand what I mean when I talk about systemic racism or even when I ask them to see me and not say they don't see color. "Be easy on people, hard on ideas" means I may understand their intentions, but I still get to challenge their thinking and allow myself to converse in a way that teaches, even when I'm tired of teaching. It's tiring to have to constantly prove your existence is worth equality and dignity. But the way I see it, I'm teaching others how to treat me and those who look like me, not just for me but for all those coming after me and for those who are rightfully too exhausted to teach anymore.

"Be easy on people, hard on ideas" means even when someone is doing something as an ally, but their allyship is performative, we can have a conversation about what they did that didn't work versus who they are. This is so much better for everyone involved. It removes the attack on their character and keeps the attention on the idea behind the action.

"Be easy on people, hard on ideas" means writing this book. Challenging the ideas that cause me and other Black people, Indigenous people, and people of color harm doesn't mean we don't challenge, it means we challenge with dignity for the sake of our own dignity.

WORK AND COMMUNITY

After we examine our relationships with friends and family it is natural to turn to our work and community. But truthfully, this may happen simultaneously. Our work lives and our community lives are intricately connected to who we are, which is why they must be places where we feel seen, heard, liked, and maybe even loved. Our workplace and our communities are also where we can feel extremely vulnerable. But here's the beauty in that vulnerability, in that discomfort: When we choose to make the workplace better, to make our communities better, to lead with courageous discomfort, we change the world.

If I See Something, When Do I Say Something?

DIANE

I have an African American friend who I met in my twenties when I lived in New York City. When she talked about the racism she experienced, I really thought she was exaggerating. One day she told me to watch in an apartment doorway as she tried to get a taxi. I watched as she tried to hail taxi after taxi and they would just pass her by. Then I walked out and two stopped for me right away. We worked together at a Fifth Avenue department store and there was a policy to have our bags checked at the end of our workday. One day, as we were just getting off work, we were so caught up in conversation that we forgot to get our bags checked. The next day at work, the management called only her into the security office to tell her they were writing her up and giving her a performance improvement plan because she didn't get her purse checked before leaving for the day. When I told them that I hadn't had my purse checked either, they said, "We don't know if you did," implying that it didn't matter. So, she got written up and I didn't. I saw it as them giving me a white pass. I told management you have to write me up too and they did. My friend was grateful that I was there and advocated for her, but seeing things like this changed my life.

Use your voice, even if it shakes.

What's Really Going On

What Diane did by speaking up to management couldn't have been easy. In a few moments, Diane had to process a lot of information, feel her emotions, and decide what action she would take as a result. Specifically, Diane had to quickly assess that 1) her friend was being treated differently than she was due to her race and then 2) decide if she was going to point out that difference to her superiors. That took courage because she could easily have stayed silent. And many of us have gotten the message that there's no point in getting involved. Whatever you hear or see, it's better to keep out of other people's business.

The simple definition of a *bystander* is a person who's present at an event but doesn't take part. In reality, bystanding is a lot more complicated. It can be doing or saying nothing, or laughing nervously when racism happens in all kinds of ways with all kinds of people. It happens with parents when they drive carpool and hear one of the kids say a racist joke, but they don't say anything because they fear that their child will suffer social consequences if they do. It happens while you're waiting in line at the grocery store, and someone white says something snarky about the Black, Indigenous, or person of color who's taking a long time to check out. It happens when we read people's posts online and get upset but don't say anything to them about it, ever. It happens when we hear a friend saying something horrible and we laugh, not because we think they're funny, but because we're nervous, and our laughter looks like we think someone else's degradation is entertaining.

Sometimes bystanders are convinced to join the person abusing power because they don't want to make things uncomfortable for themselves. They don't want the aggressor setting their sights on them because it's easier for people to default to automatic responses like freezing or running away. Bystanders can be silent, and their apparent neutrality looks like support for what the bully is doing.

Standing in solidarity with her friend meant Diane could have faced consequences for speaking out. She could have gotten fired. Even the possibility of being fired or getting punished in some way stops many people from advocating for people's dignity in moments like these—the moments they are needed most.

THINK ABOUT IT
We've all been a bystander in a situation where we should have spoken up. What was your reason for making that choice?

A Better Approach

Contrary to how easy people can make it seem (usually when they aren't involved), it's never easy going from being a bystander to a person who chooses to speak out. Far from it. Speaking out when people are trying to take away the dignity of another can be terrifying. We all know this. We know it like we know how to breathe. We don't even need to say it to ourselves, we just get the feeling of fear and being overwhelmed.

That's why we so easily convince ourselves not to believe what is happening before our eyes because then we may ask ourselves what, if anything, we should do. The first thing you can do is simple: Acknowledge that "it" will happen; we all will have moments when we will see someone do or say something racist, and we'll have to decide what to do about it. The more you accept that fact and ask yourself how you want to show up and why, the better you'll be able to handle whatever situation you find yourself in and in a way you can be proud of.

When you feel incapacitated by your emotional reaction to the things you sense or experience around you, you are experiencing *emotional hijacking*. When you are emotionally hijacked, you can't think clearly. Your brain goes into automatic reactive mode, and that means your response can easily default to how you were raised to react to stress or conflict. This is why so many of us freeze in these moments. Unfortunately, this can often look like we are in denial, and this can keep us from helping the vulnerable person who needs us most. It can be confusing, overwhelming, and it can leave us feeling ashamed (if we can even admit that our emotions stopped us from reacting as we would have wanted).

You will know you're in a bystanding moment because

you'll say something to yourself like, *Is this really happening right now?* or you will feel your heart beat faster or your breathing may change. When this happens, slow down, take a breath, and pay attention to what you are seeing and feeling.

Next, check that you are physically safe and then remind yourself that you are safe. Then, look for the most concrete way you can affirm this targeted person's dignity. Remember, it doesn't have to be a grand gesture. Diane telling her supervisors that she also didn't have her bag checked and should be disciplined in the same way wasn't starting an anti-racist campaign at work for everyone to see. It simply forced the people with power to understand that Diane perceived their behavior as racist in the moment that it was happening. If she hadn't said anything, it could look like she agreed with her supervisors or didn't have the personal fortitude to speak out. Either way, they would have believed she was on their "side."

Your goal is to move yourself from being a bystander who is controlled by the dynamics around you to a person who contributes to affirming the dignity of the person being dehumanized.

In these moments, think of yourself as the kid on the playground reaching out to the child who is being hurt by another student. You recognize the moment when some kind of intervention is necessary to affirm the dignity and/or physical safety of the target(s), and then act. That action can take different forms:

You pay attention to the dynamic that is stripping the target of their dignity.

You acknowledge what's happening.

You affirm the target's dignity.

You do everything you can to reinforce the target's emotional and physical safety.

If you see something, when do you say something?
As soon as you realize someone's dignity is at stake. This will help you make the right decision to help the situation.

Meditate on It
Have you ever been in a situation where you wanted to help but didn't? What stopped you?

If you could go back in time and redo how you responded in the situation, what would you do differently?

KEY TAKEAWAYS

- Emotional hijacking is the experience of being captured by your emotional reaction to the things you sense or experience around you.

- Your goal is to transform yourself from a bystander who is controlled by the dynamics around you to a person who contributes to affirming the dignity of the person being dehumanized.

- Yes, there may be consequences for speaking out that may make your life more difficult. It's OK to admit that. But it's important to consider that the consequences of going through life not speaking out, and letting others speak for you, takes away your own dignity and your sense of self-worth.

Does It Always Have to Be about Race?

AVA

I struggled to get along with a Black woman in my office. She was someone who complained quite a bit and never gave suggestions for how to make things better. I talked to her to understand how we could work together differently. I was her supervisor, and I knew celebrating birthdays and other holidays was important to her, so I did my best to show appreciation for her on those days. Cards, flowers, call outs for her good work in meetings. Unfortunately, my efforts were never enough for her. At the same time, I was having serious health problems. I was exhausted and working hard to keep up. She knew some of the things I was dealing with personally, but my needs didn't compare to hers. I felt I couldn't say anything about these things because I'm white and her boss. I don't care what race she is, I was just relieved when she left to take another job.

You don't have to like everyone, just check your assumptions first.

What's Really Going On

Of course people can get on your last nerve for all kinds of reasons that have nothing to do with race. Maybe they never stop talking, or they're flaky with plans, or they're rude to waiters, or butt in line, or talk badly about people . . . or don't say thanks after you do something nice for them like throw them a birthday party at work.

But here's the real question at the root of this story: *Can a white person dislike a person of another race and not be considered racist?*

Let's look at Ava's situation. She made the effort to know her team and what makes them feel acknowledged.

Part of knowing her team is knowing that birthdays are very important to this team member. Ava is also hyper-aware of the power and privilege she has in relation to this team member. She is 1) white, 2) her boss, and therefore 3) earns more money. She's so aware that it actually makes it more difficult for her to admit that she just doesn't like her employee as a person, and so avoids asking for what she wants and deserves, which is to be treated with the same dignity she's putting forward.

So, let's go back to our question. Of course Ava doesn't have to like this team member. Trying to be nice to someone, acknowledging what's important to them and still, no expression of gratitude? Ava's particular situation is complicated by the power dynamic inherent in a manager/employee relationship, and race makes it extra hard. It's difficult to put yourself out there for someone repeatedly without any expression of gratitude, regardless of whether it happens in your personal or professional life. And while the parties in this story are of different races, this dislike is not inherently racist or prejudiced.

Here's why.

Prejudice refers to a preconceived opinion or feeling toward a person based solely on their affiliation with a group. Which means, you can dislike someone based on their behavior, character, principles, or how they show up in the world. But that doesn't mean you judge someone ahead of knowing anything about them solely because they may have the same racial identity as someone you dislike. When we do, then we're being prejudiced. If Ava took her experience with this one colleague and concluded that all Black women would be unappreciative or ignore her feelings, and therefore, she doesn't want to work with or even like Black women in general, then she would be prejudiced and racist.

This may seem obvious, but it needs to be said: All Black people don't invite all other Black people to social events, gatherings, or to their homes (in other words, all Black people are not invited to the cookout). All people of color don't get along with one another. All white people don't automatically like all other white people. No matter what race you are, you don't have to like someone whose behavior and character don't align with your own.

THINK ABOUT IT
When was the last time someone annoyed you and you checked your reasons for being annoyed?

A Better Approach

While this principle is straightforward, it's often hard to put into practice because we are all constantly assessing other people and their behavior, and then analyzing these assessments. All the time. How we interpret others' actions is based on our own personal filter, and that is where we can check ourselves.

Imagine waiting in a line or getting customer support and getting annoyed with the person helping you: What story are you telling yourself in this situation? Are you telling yourself that this person is being unhelpful and now they are getting on your last nerve or is it this [insert someone's race] person being unhelpful and not only are they getting on your last nerve, but this proves or reinforces that these people are X and always X? See? There is a big difference there—a really big difference.

Once you realize the why and how of your feelings toward this other person, own it to yourself (you don't have to explain anything to the other person) and give the other person a break. Meaning, just describe them to yourself as an annoying person and that's it. Then take a deep breath and calmly tell the person what you need.

Before you decide "I don't like/trust/think this person is cool," take a few moments to ask yourself a couple questions:

What assumptions am I making about this person?

What story am I telling myself about this person?

Are any of the reasons why I like or dislike this person really about what's going on with me?

Meditate on It

Have you ever felt obligated to convince yourself that you liked someone of a different race?

Do you know someone of a different race that you don't like?

Have you somehow connected how you feel about them with their race?

KEY TAKEAWAYS

- You always have the right to not like someone; just check in with yourself about any biases that could influence your judgment.

- You aren't a bad person for having any of these feelings.

- Even if you don't like the person, treating them with dignity should always be your baseline.

What's the Harm in Being Curious?

SHANTERRA

Once upon a time, I lived in the Bay Area. I loved the Bay, but I always looked forward to visiting my family in my hometown of Dallas. Another highlight of these trips, in addition to seeing my family, was the chance to catch up and have lunch with my BFF4L (Best Friend Forever for Life), Talisha.

On one of my visits, Talisha asked me to accompany her to an essential oils party at her chiropractor's office. When we arrived at the party, I immediately gave it "the scan"—when you, as a person of color, look around to see if anyone else looks like you—and realized Talisha and I were the only two Black people in the space. ("Yes," we said to one another, "we're the only two.")

Another important part of the scan includes noting the stares from white people, to which you (the person of color) give a smile and nod to imply, *Yes, I'm friendly and yes, I belong here.* The intention of the stares varies, but I pay attention to the smiles responding to my smile: Sometimes there's a genuinely welcoming smile, sometimes there's the overly enthusiastic welcome (an excited "Hiiiiii-iii") to let me know they are a safe and friendly white person.

Don't get me wrong. I'm not saying that being very excited to see me is *bad*. It's just that I'm always assessing reactions, both mine and others, when I'm in a room full of people who don't look like me. If I don't respond with the same level of enthusiasm, I wonder if the white person will assume that I'm unfriendly or not supposed to be there. If I do respond with the same level of enthusiasm, will that prove that I'm friendly or I'm where I'm supposed to be? I shouldn't have to think about these things, but I do.

When the social ended, the doctor's office was abuzz with people interested in this new essential oil lifestyle, me included. As I was sitting in a chair completing paperwork, I felt something in my hair. I brushed away whatever had landed on me and went back to the task. A few minutes passed and again, I felt something in my hair. This time it had made its way *into* my hair and was touching my scalp. I turned around quickly, only to see a surprised white woman pull her hand away from my hair.

"Why are you touching me?" I asked the woman.

"I just wanted to see what *it* felt like. It looks so soft," she replied.

I said, incredulously, "What?"

Then the tears came . . . from her.

Our interaction caused enough of a stir that another white woman came over to us and asked *her* what happened. The crying woman responded, through her tears, "I just wanted to touch her hair and, and . . ." More tears.

The rescuer wrapped her arms around the upset woman, looked at me disappointedly, and said, "She didn't mean any harm. She was just *curious*," and continued to console her.

That's when I knew I needed to quickly get out of the party because this was no longer a safe space for me. I had expressed my irritation at being touched without my consent and was immediately perceived as wrong or irrational by these women. They felt that they had the right to say and do what they wanted to me, and any reaction besides my acceptance was intolerable to them.

Yep, I felt irritated because as much as I was surprised that a total stranger had her hand in my hair, when I turned around and saw her look of fear, I knew *I* would have to take the high road in this situation even though *she* was the one who touched *me*. Taking the high road was for my own safety; it had nothing to do with her. As a person of color, you learn and hear quite often, when they go low, we go high, even when you're extremely irritated.

No matter how curious you are, touching requires consent.

What's Really Going On

If the woman had touched Shanterra anywhere else on her body, such as her face or her breast, you could understand how the woman crossed the line because there is a presumption that people do not want others, especially those who do not know them intimately, to touch their bodies without consent. Touching the hand, arm, or shoulder may be socially acceptable until someone says stop or pulls away.

When a white person touches any Black woman's hair because she is *curious* and because *it looks so soft*, this is a violation of the Black woman's personal space. We know some will think this sounds harsh, especially because the woman seemed genuinely curious, and then hurt, by the interaction. But what may be even harder to accept is that when Shanterra speaks out to protect herself, she feels like she is putting herself in danger.

Yes, we know "danger" may sound overly intense, but put yourself in Shanterra's place. She didn't know the woman. They didn't have a relationship built on trust and intimacy that would have made touching acceptable. Touching hair is intimate and should be presumed unwelcomed, especially when it's coming from a stranger. When the woman started to cry, it implied that Shanterra had violated the woman instead of the other way around.

Unfortunately, Shanterra is not alone in her experience. Many Black people have stories like this, where a white person, usually a woman, touches their hair without permission. If it's not touched, it's commented on, it's stared at, it's talked about.

But isn't it just hair?

As a woman, when your body is touched by a total stranger, one of the first things you do is try to make sense of it. You look for a rational reason that would make the whole thing a big misunderstanding, while knowing full well there's no way to misunderstand what happened. In this scenario at the essential oils party, there's a power dynamic at play here, and this is not just about hair. It's about feeling ownership over another's body and believing curiosity overrides someone's bodily autonomy.

This woman didn't believe Shanterra had the right to have her body respected. Instead, she believed her curiosity gave her the right to examine Shanterra without regard for her feelings.

OK, here is where you may get a bit uncomfortable, but we have to say the hard thing so we can be a part of creating the world we all want to be proud of and feel safe in.

It's common to hear, *slavery was so long ago*. We hear this a lot, especially when a Black person earns a big position and has attained wealth or to justify no longer needing to celebrate Black History Month. *Slavery was so long ago* denies the very real impact it has on Black people to this day.

When slavery was still prevalent, white women would

examine enslaved Black women on auction blocks as they were being sold away from their families. White people would turn a Black woman around to see her size and stature, have her open her mouth and look at her teeth and gums, and touch her hair, all because enslaved Black women were viewed as property. The enslaved Black woman on the auction block couldn't say, "Why are you touching me?" regardless of how degraded she felt. Regardless of how scared she was, she had to accept her degradation to stay alive. White supremacy, including slavery, meant a Black woman's life, and body, was not her own.

It may seem like a stretch to white women to state that the woman who touched Shanterra's hair out of curiosity was doing so for similar reasons, but nevertheless, it triggers a deeply rooted generational trauma. Shanterra's experience demonstrates the seemingly small, but powerful, ways Black women are reminded that white people don't believe Black people's bodies are their own. And if you're not allowed to see your body as your own, you're also not allowed to feel annoyed or frustrated about having it touched without invitation either.

Believing you have the right to touch a Black woman's hair, especially without her consent, is equivalent to not seeing a Black woman as a person. If you're really seeing a Black woman as a person, you would stop and think, *Wait, I don't have the right to touch her without her invitation.*

Are you saying if the woman had asked Shanterra if she could touch her hair, that would have been OK?

No! It's a no-win situation. Even if this question comes from a place of curiosity, it presumes that the woman feels like she has the *right to ask*, which is another byproduct of white supremacy. In other words, white supremacy says, "I'm asking, however, the permission to touch is already mine." The person has to say yes or they're not being amenable, being cooperative, or catering to the white person's interest or needs. Even if the woman wasn't aware of the root of her actions, she benefits from that privilege. We know this because a stranger defended her right to be curious. In reality, a white woman asking to touch a Black woman's hair is dehumanizing and puts her in a

position of feeling unsafe if she doesn't agree to her own dehumanization.

THINK ABOUT IT
Has anyone ever been curious about you in a way that made you uncomfortable?

A Better Approach
While the angry Black woman stereotype (something we get into more in the next chapter, see page 208) can be used to invalidate a Black woman's lived experience, it can also be used to keep Black women "in their place." Shanterra was rightfully angry, but she had to minimize how she expressed her anger because otherwise her reaction would be perceived as out of control and unreasonable. When that happens, some white

people feel entitled to do whatever they need to do to feel safe, including not seeing the context in which they are operating. Shanterra and other Black women know this, so in that moment, Shanterra had to decide how to respond so the other women wouldn't consider her a threat—even though she had to compromise her dignity to do it.

The way the woman responded to Shanterra's rightful annoyance also helped solidify the racial power dynamics in the room. When Shanterra asked the woman why she was touching her, the woman didn't reply with words, she responded with tears. The tears could have been because she was caught off guard or she was embarrassed. But, at that moment, her tears were interpreted by another woman in the space as a cry for help.

While it's healthy to cry when you are sad, frustrated, or upset and need to release your feelings, sometimes people use crying to get out of trouble and solicit other people's protection. In this case, whether it was purposeful or not, the woman's crying manipulated the other white women in the room into eliciting sympathy for her so she wouldn't be held accountable. Crying shifted the attention and blame away from her actions to Shanterra's reaction, so that Shanterra became the problem. It's precisely during these incidents when the Black woman who is on the receiving end of whatever bad thing is happening to them is acutely aware that if they make "too much" of a situation, they will reinforce the stereotype of the angry Black woman and put their emotional and physical safety at risk.

What do you do if you make a mistake like this? Instead of giving a bunch of different what ifs, we're going straight to the suggestions and sentence scripts you can use to guide your words.

Own it and apologize.
Short and sweet apology: *I'm so sorry I* [say what you did].

Longer version: *I'm so sorry I* [say what you did]. *I hear you and I apologize. I need to reflect on why I thought it was OK to do.*

If someone comes to your rescue:
You say: *I have misread the situation. I am the one at fault and I need to apologize for my thoughtlessness.*

If your friend made the mistake:
Don't rescue your friend. You are supporting them when you have them acknowledge the dignity of the person they have wronged. That might sound like, *Please don't touch this woman's hair.* If you are witnessing someone not being treated with dignity, don't worry, a person of color will not be angry with you for speaking out.

We want to draw your attention to why we are suggesting a declarative statement instead of doing what is more common and asking "Why are you touching her hair?" Sometimes, like here, questions aren't questions. You don't want to get into a discussion with the person about the "why"; you'll have much more success later when you are one-on-one and can ask a curious question. That's when you can say, *Hey, I'd like to talk to you about why you touched this woman's hair.*

Too often, when a white person sees rude behavior directed toward a person of color, they think, *Well, they're strong, they look like they're handling it* or *It's not my place* or *I'll just say something to her after it's over.* That isn't as helpful as addressing it in the moment. Yes, as a white person you are walking a delicate line here. You don't want to rescue the person of color, but you can't just do nothing because your inaction will look like you agree. So, you can say, *Excuse me, but from what I am seeing, you shouldn't touch this woman.* And if you're thinking right now, there's no way I could do that—that's way too uncomfortable or you don't want to cause a scene—think about what it's like for BIPOC. We can't put all this weight on their shoulders. We also must speak out because if we don't, it's too easy for this situation to devolve into an "us" (white, reasonable, harmless, just curious) vs. "them" (BIPOC, difficult, dangerous) situation. We must stand on the side of what's right, not on the side of those who may look like us.

Meditate on It
How do you react when someone is angry around you?

Does your reaction differ depending on the person's race or gender?

KEY TAKEAWAYS

- The seemingly small experiences like the story in this chapter aren't small. They tie us to the legacy of slavery, oppression, and discrimination and how it impacts interactions between white and Black people to this day.

- Touching requires consent.

- Asking for consent treats a person with dignity.

- Don't ask for consent to touch a Black person's hair. Period.

Why Are Black Women So Angry?

BROOKLYN

I first heard of the "angry Black woman" stereotype in grad school when I was 21. We were assigned a group project, and I was partnered with a Black woman (Debra) and a white man (Sam). Sam was not pulling his weight, and he spoke to the two of us like we were idiots. Debra and I were fed up and met to talk about it and make a plan. We wrote out our concerns, feedback, and requests, and even though she was the one to type them up on her computer, as she was a much stronger and more compassionate writer and clearer at expressing our needs, she asked me if I could be the one to send it to him. I asked her why, and she said she didn't want to come across as the "angry black woman." I had never heard that term, so I asked her to explain. My jaw was on the floor as she defined and shared examples. We got a positive and respectful response from Sam, which she believed, from experience, that we would not have gotten if she had sent it. I was sick to my stomach that there were so many hurdles for her, and something as seemingly small as giving a classmate feedback, and standing up for herself, came with so many considerations, energy, tiptoeing around someone else—all to get what she deserved.

Be aware of stereotypes that deny people's right to express anger.

What's Really Going On

Can you imagine what it feels like to have to ask someone to communicate for you? To speak for you and represent you because history has shown that if you use your voice, especially when criticizing a white person or speaking up for yourself, you will be ostracized and labeled difficult and angry? To know that you have to be strategic and careful when protecting your dignity because someone believes the color of your skin means you're not worthy of it?

Anger is an emotion we all experience and yet, it can be so challenging to truly understand its role in our life. Not only for you, but for the people around you. But if we get more clarity around it, we can understand ourselves and our interactions a lot better. The starting place is getting clear about its definition. Anger's goal is to force us to pay attention when we are facing a physical or psychological threat and then act to increase our physical and psychological safety. But our brains can struggle to know the difference between a real and perceived threat. The more we think our world is a hostile place, the more likely we are to identify a threat when it may not be there. Think of a young man on a basketball court who freaks out because someone accidentally ran into him and his ego is threatened, or a parent at a school board meeting who is up in arms and having a self-righteous temper tantrum, or a news celebrity who rages when someone disagrees with them on air. None of these people are facing a physical threat, yet their actions suggest otherwise and then make other people angry, so the whole thing escalates.

Making this even more challenging is how each of us is "allowed" to express our anger. Because make no mistake, one of the most powerful unwritten rules of our culture is who is allowed to express anger openly and what happens if we break this rule.

The truth is, how people are taught and allowed to express anger doesn't operate on a level or fair playing field. When you have more status (i.e., power), you have more freedom to express your anger any way you choose. Conversely,

the less power you have, the more you learn to hide your anger because if you express it, you will be punished: You'll be dismissed, ridiculed, made to feel guilty, or seen as the problem and then disproportionately punished. Think of Sandra Bland and her anger at the police officer because she was pulled over for failure to signal a lane change and how the police officer escalated his response. He didn't escalate because of the gravity of her crime, he did so because she was angry about how he was treating her and he didn't believe she had the right to express that anger.

Let's step away from race for a moment and look at gender. Think about the way we expect and allow men to express their anger. During all the years we have worked, we have met countless men who didn't want to grow up to be angry like the men they grew up with. We both have known many men who have said to us, "I hate being angry because I don't want to be like my dad." But there are also many men who feel that they have the right, a right they don't even think about, to express their anger however they want.

Now think about how women are taught to express their anger. As women, we often try to push our anger away because it's an emotion we don't feel entitled to claim. We are often taught to express anger in passive-aggressive ways or wait for people to read our minds about how we really feel. Then we hide how angry we are when their mind reading is off, and they miss what we're really angry about.

Now let's fold race into how people perceive *how* they can express their anger. In an equitable society, how people are taught and given permission to express their anger should not have race attached to it, but that's our reality. Every culture has rules and social expectations about how people should and shouldn't express feelings, and then folds racial stereotypes and bias into what different people are allowed to do. For our purposes—and because this book can't be a thousand pages long—we will focus on Black women's anger, but think about how Latina women's anger is often labeled "spicy" and "fiery," and if you're Asian American or Pacific Islander, the cultural rule is to always stay calm no matter how angry you are.

For women of color, especially Black women, the cultural rules of expressing anger are intricate and oppressive. If a Black woman uses her voice in an authoritative manner or she shows any negative emotion, she's "yelling" and told to "calm down." Black women experience this in the workplace, in the grocery store, in their neighborhoods, on the playground, on airplanes, in the shopping mall, anywhere they are in public. This is the air they breathe.

They are labeled the angry Black woman, even when they aren't angry. Even when they have every right to be.

Are you familiar with the term *angry Black woman*? The label has been in existence for a long time and was invented to normalize the belief that Black women were loud, sassy, and aggressive—completely contrary to how Black women were allowed to be. It originated from a racist caricature: a Black woman called Sapphire. It started shortly after the Civil War in the late 1800s when Jim Crow laws were spreading throughout the South to strip financial, political, and social freedoms Black people gained after emancipation. This is when the signs for "Colored Only" or "White People Only" became a normal, accepted practice in communities around the country. One of the strategies to make these laws and policies acceptable was to create archetypes of Black people that would rationalize these practices to the white public. Sapphire was one of them.

Sapphire existed for generations after that and became

part of the American cultural landscape as one of the main characters in the immensely popular CBS television program *The Amos 'n' Andy Show.* Airing from 1951 to 1953 with an all-Black cast, the show's main characters were Sapphire Stevens and her husband George "Kingfish" Stevens, who was always depicted as ignorant and lazy. Sapphire raged at Kingfish and chastised white people in the show as if she had real power and equality, regardless of the fact that if a Black woman acted that way in real life, she would have risked her life. Sapphire perpetuated this depiction of Black women, so it was continually reinforced and spread in the culture through the new medium of television.

The Sapphire caricature exists today in many movies and television shows, including any Real Housewives of any city featuring Black women. We see it when Black women try to explain their experiences of racism in the media and white people accuse them of being angry or crazy or a "monster." Not only does this depiction relegate Black women to entertainment, but it also reinforces the message to all of us that this is how Black women "really are." And because these images are believed, they diminish the experiences, feelings, and humanity of Black women in real life.

All this is in Black women's minds every time they are angry, so they must filter their feelings to be palatable to the white people around them and to the institutions they are trying to navigate. That's why so many Black women have stories like Debra's—fear that a white person will not take her seriously or will feel threatened when she expresses anything other than happiness or gratitude.

THINK ABOUT IT
Have you ever had your anger dismissed? What did you do?

A Better Approach
Yes, that was a lot to get us to this point of understanding what happened between Brooklyn and Debra, but it was necessary. Debra didn't make the decision lightly to confide in Brooklyn and ask her to send the email to their colleague on their behalf. It took courage to build her trust in Brooklyn, which was based on watching, listening, and interacting with Brooklyn. Debra also had to trust that Brooklyn wouldn't out her

to Sam. In other words, she trusted Brooklyn would treat her with dignity and act as an ally. For Debra, that's a whole lot of trust.

After working with Debra on their talking points and the email, Brooklyn shared how she was surprised that Debra would ask her to send the email to Sam. Although Debra asked for her assistance, Brooklyn now understood that Debra wasn't asking to be rescued or for Brooklyn to be the white savior, which is sometimes how allyship can be interpreted. Debra wasn't asking Brooklyn to feel sorry for her and she wasn't trying to not pull her weight. She just knew the message to Sam needed to come from Brooklyn for it to be better received and therefore get what they wanted accomplished.

If you are ever in a position like Brooklyn's, the most important way you can show up better is to believe Black women and all women of color when they say they are angry, and/or when they perceive the angry label may be put upon them. And for all of the women's empowerment, you-deserve-to-speak-your-truth, your-voice-matters, don't-let-them-silence-you, you-deserve-to-be-heard people . . . we hear you, but hear us out. You're not saying anything that a Black woman or woman of color doesn't already know. We get it; aphorisms are wonderful and sometimes we all need a little encouragement or a cheerleader. But in instances where a Black woman or any woman of color's dignity is at stake, she doesn't need a cheerleader, she needs an ally. She's not sending the email or in other instances, not speaking up in the meeting or not speaking up on the call because she doesn't believe she's unworthy. Consider that she may not be speaking up because she has experiences with people that have shown her that *they* don't believe she's worthy. As an ally, here's an opportunity to advocate with and for her on her behalf.

How can I advocate for a Black woman or any person of color in a situation like this?
First: Listen! Be prepared to be changed by what you hear! Brooklyn handled this well: When Debra brought up her discomfort, Brooklyn asked why, listened to the reason, and believed Debra without any further justification. Her compassion and belief were what Debra needed. And how else did Brooklyn not screw it up? She didn't force Debra

to confront the system or to confront Sam on her own.

In the first chapter (see page 38), we talked about what it means to be an ally, so you know now that being an ally doesn't mean you have to relate to someone's experience. Being an ally means:

1. You believe the other person's experience, and you acknowledge that it is wrong.

2. You act on your belief.

That's exactly what Brooklyn did.

But is that enough? Should someone talk to Sam? If so, who should that be?
Sam didn't realize any of this was going on behind the scenes. Should someone tell him what's going on? Many years ago, these are the questions Rosalind would have asked. It wouldn't have been enough to be the ally to Debra. She would have had to make sure Sam learned his lesson. She would have had to make sure he knew how he was contributing to the silence and disempowerment of a woman of color. It would have been a whole scene. What's even worse, she would have asked Debra if she could talk to Sam. And Debra would have told her, no, that it wasn't necessary because she didn't want to get caught in Rosalind's self-righteous crusade and Rosalind still would have talked to him. It would have pissed off Debra because it wouldn't have been about the silence and disempowerment of a woman of color. It would have been all about Rosalind and making her feel affirmed. But Rosalind's needs aren't the point here. Debra's are.

It's important to ask if talking to Sam would make things better or worse. Not for you but for the person who is already marginalized. So, if Debra does say no, hold tight because it is probable that you will personally experience Sam repeating this behavior. Therefore, you want to be prepared if and when he does. To do that, ask yourself these questions: What specifically do you want to say? What request do you have of him? And how do you want to handle it if he gets defensive?

As an ally, it makes sense that you would want to have a conversation with Sam about his behavior. Having a preexisting relationship may give you a better chance that he will listen. Don't get distracted by or caught up in the word "ally." If treating people with dignity is at the forefront of your mind, people will respond. It doesn't matter if it's someone in Debra's position or Sam's. Being an ally means you are the verb. Lead with dignity.

Meditate on It

How do you respond differently to a person's anger if they are a different race than you?

How has the stereotype of the "angry Black woman" influenced your perceptions of Black women?

KEY TAKEAWAYS

- Labels, stereotypes, and caricatures have power. It's important to know where they came from to understand their influence on you and people around you.

- Anger is a powerful emotion and very few of us are allowed to express it without other people demeaning it and dismissing it.

- How to express or not express anger may not be in your head all the time, but it is always in the head of Black women.

Why Can't I Just Do My Job?

KIMBERLY

Our company had contributed to improving a public land project that children in the community could use, but because we contributed, we also wanted preferential access to use the land. And that meant that Black and brown kids from the Boys and Girls Clubs would just stand around having to wait until a lot of white people finished. This issue was being brought up in community meetings, so my manager came to me and said, "We need diversity at the meeting and because you're African American, I'm sure you have no problem being at the meeting." I said I couldn't testify at the meeting because I wasn't a resident, which she knew. Although it disturbed me, I didn't address it, then. I didn't say anything because in my mind, I have a rubric and I judge the micro-aggressions depending on how egregious they are and what else is going on the rest of the day for me personally. It's not anything written down, I just keep it in my head. There were always tears with her and I didn't feel like dealing with them. The next day I was in a meeting with my CEO about something totally different. But before getting to the reason we were meeting, she made a point to thank me for attending the community meeting and for being "a team player." I just couldn't let that slide. So although I wasn't prepared to say anything to her I said, "In the future, I want to be asked to attend a meeting because I have something to contribute, not because I'm Black." She vehemently disagreed and said my manager got it wrong and said it was about wanting different departments represented, but that wasn't true. Then she apologized for my manager and said she was stressed, she had a lot going on, and my being Black was not the reason I was asked to attend and clearly, my manager misunderstood. I reminded her that this is not the first time something like this had occurred where my race was used for optics. Then she suggested I talk to my manager. I told her I'd rather not because she avoids conflict, freezes, or *she'll start crying and then I'll have to figure out how to manage her tears.*

THINK ABOUT IT
Have you had someone take away your dignity at work and you felt like there was nothing you could do about it?

Have the courage to question your emotional "truth."

What's Going On

Where do we begin? Well, let's start with just taking a moment to imagine what it would feel like to be Kimberly. Your manager "invites" you to a work event that you don't feel you can decline. She invites you, not because of your experience and intellect, but so you can help your company maintain a superficial image of diversity and community service. You are reluctant to tell your manager who put you in this situation because she'll get upset and then you'll have to take care of her. Then your CEO gaslights you by presenting "alternative facts" that you know aren't true, but fit the false narrative about why you participated in this charade in the first place. At the same time, you have a career to maintain, children to take care of, and bills to pay. You can't risk getting the reputation for being difficult or angry (cue all the baggage we already talked about in the last chapter). And . . . you still take the risk of telling the CEO what you really think. Anyone else have a major headache coming on?

Did you notice how Kimberly referenced her microaggression rubric? She decided that being asked to attend a meeting wasn't egregious enough at that moment to make a fuss about it. Kimberly made that decision because she didn't want to deal with a manager who couldn't handle conflict beyond avoiding it, freezing, or crying.

In the last chapter, we talked about how Black women are hyperaware of their tone, especially at work, especially when talking to white people. The reason Kimberly decided to speak out when the CEO brought it up was because at that point, she recognized that the CEO's "thanks" was really a way to cover up what had happened. If Kimberly didn't say anything at that moment, the CEO would then have the story she needed, and Kimberly would lose the only power she had in that situation: to describe how she had been used. Even then, Kimberly had to communicate all of this diplomatically because she couldn't come across as angry, out of control, or unprofessional—even though what had been asked of her was unethical. Making it worse, the CEO simultaneously undermined Kimberly by making excuses for her manager's actions.

But didn't this all begin with Kimberly's manager? Wasn't she "just being honest" when she told Kimberly why she wanted her to attend the public hearing? Yes, but she should never have asked her to do it in the first place. Asking someone to do anything because of how it would look favorable for the company is tokenism. Tokenism looks like a commitment to diversity, but it's actually a way to reinforce the unequal power dynamics that support discrimination and an unsafe work environment. And when that was brought to her attention, she didn't want to believe it.

For both the manager and the CEO, in the moment when they were confronted with understanding their real motivations, they chose to deny it. And that makes this workplace unsafe for Kimberly to work in, let alone do her job well.

THINK ABOUT IT
Have you or a colleague ever been asked to attend a meeting, speak up in a meeting, be in company photos for the website, or even serve on the Diversity, Equity, and Inclusion committees for optics?

A Better Approach

Yes, the manager shouldn't have done it in the first place. But we've all done things we realize only later were mistakes. So, let's take it from that moment: How do you move forward when you have to repair the situation? You ask yourself the following:

What blinded me from seeing that my request would be inappropriate?

Was there any part of me that knew it though I chose not to listen?

What did I say to myself to justify that asking this person, or putting this person in a situation to be a token, was appropriate?

What was my justification hiding or rationalizing?

What is making me feel vulnerable in this situation?

How can I work to restore dignity to this person?

The way in which the CEO wanted to calm the conflict down was to present "alternative facts" even though Kimberly knew the truth from her manager. In situations like this, it seems easier to deny the truth instead of owning what is really going on. Attempting to present an alternative truth is never a good idea. You lose credibility for yourself and credibility with your colleagues when you deny what's really happening.

So many people of color just want to go to work and do their job. They don't want to be, or feel obligated to be, on committees for diversity, equity, and inclusion. They don't want to feel responsible for having to call out bad behavior. They certainly don't want to be anyone's token.

Meditate on It
Picture yourself at a meeting where a supervisor asks a person of color to participate in something that is clearly only because of their race. What would you do?

KEY TAKEAWAYS

- Tokenism, on the surface, may look like people of color are included and represented, but it never does to the people of color who know they are being used to present a false front.

- If you make a mistake, ask yourself what blinded you from seeing that you were treating someone as a token.

- Our motivation to do the right thing and speak up when our work culture doesn't match the principles that it stands for is not about one person. Speaking up is about creating a culture where everyone feels safe, heard, and valued.

Can't I Do Anything Right?

ROSALIND

A few years ago, Shanterra and I were co-facilitating a professional development training program with one hundred teachers in Dallas, Texas. After I finished up my section, I turned it over to Shanterra to lead the next module. Shanterra walked to the front of the big training room with whiteboards at her back and a racially diverse group of teachers sitting in a big U shape facing her. As soon as she began, I went to the back of the room and sat on a raised counter that ran the length of the back of the room. As she spoke, I sat on the counter and wrote notes, so my head was down. I remember choosing to sit in the back because I wanted to give her the entire spotlight.

After her portion was over and the teachers went to lunch, I walked up to Shanterra with a smile, only to be met with "the look." It's a look I prefer not to have focused in my direction, but there it was, unmistakably. I remember feeling confused that she was angry with me, and even more confused when she explained why: I had undermined her authority by sitting in the back of the room while she presented. Instead of acknowledging her feelings, I doubled down on my cluelessness and said things like, "Are you sure? From the way I was sitting?" which made her more irritated, and I got an even more intense look.

I'm sure my body language conveyed my confusion and defensiveness. I asked myself, *Why was she getting upset about something so small? She knows me!*

SHANTERRA

As soon as I started teaching and saw Rosalind go to the

back of the room and sit on a table with her legs crossed, I knew my authority was undermined. The teachers knew she was the lead trainer and knew her work. I knew the teachers in the room didn't know who I was or if I had any credibility.

I needed Rosalind to stay up front. Not to hover and watch over me, but to model what it looked like to accept my authority on the subject matter. Rosalind going to the back and putting her head down and "tuning me out" felt like she was being dismissive. I was concerned teachers would see that and think, *Oh, we really don't have to pay attention to her because the leader is in the back writing.*

At the end of our day, we went to dinner and talked. I shared my frustration with Rosalind, and it took a while because she didn't get it. We were approaching the situation with two different lenses and two different perspectives. But we heard each other. Truth is, Rosalind wasn't trying to tune me out or discredit me. She didn't know how to show her confidence in my ability and competence. She knew she needed to, but she thought that going to the back would send the "right" message. She wasn't being dismissive; she was trying to give me the authority in the space. By getting out of the way, she was attempting to show the teachers that "Shanterra is in charge. Trust everything she says." I wouldn't have known that if I hadn't given her the feedback to know how she was coming across.

Accepting feedback is the key to learning.

What's Really Going On

How else will we learn our blind spots if they're not pointed out? Here's what Rosalind understood in this situation: She was very aware of the challenges women often have in leadership positions (for example, you can't ask for help or else you will look incompetent). What Rosalind didn't know is how much more alive this dynamic is for women of color, and she didn't know how to show others that she was confident in Shanterra's leadership as a Black woman.

And while there are some people who love to point out other people's mistakes and give them "feedback," most people dread these moments. The reasons for this are numerous. It's always hard for people to give each other feedback, especially women because we don't want to be seen as "mean." For Shanterra, as a Black woman, even though she and Rosalind have a strong friendship and because Black women's competence is so often questioned, asking for help feels like opening the door to being seen as incompetent. Asking also means that the person may disappoint you if they don't rise to the occasion. It's easy to feel caught in a no-win situation; ask for help and you undermine your own authority. However, don't ask, don't say what you need, and watch even your good friend cluelessly undermine your authority.

This is what Rosalind realized when Shanterra told her how upset she was: 1) Shanterra would never say she was upset unless she really was. 2) It didn't matter that Rosalind didn't mean to be disrespectful, that's how Shanterra felt so that's what counted. 3) As a white woman, Rosalind didn't understand the dynamics in the room for Shanterra; and 4) as her partner, Rosalind had a responsibility to support her and her position of leadership as a Black woman.

THINK ABOUT IT

Think of the last time someone gave you negative feedback. How did you respond? What did you learn from that experience?

A Better Approach

It's all too easy to get defensive when we get negative feedback. It's natural. It's understandable. But when we respond defensively, we lose opportunities to grow and become cooler people. We also lose the opportunity to acknowledge and apologize for whatever we did that hurt the other person.

Our world is desperate for all of us to get better at accepting when we mess up. When someone gives you feedback, you have to just feel your feelings and remember that they will pass if you let them. If you let them pass through you, you can process them and understand what happened much better. If you don't, you are likely to be stuck in resentment and the need to be right. And needing to be right is a great way to lose relationships.

Then ask yourself two questions:

What was the most important thing this person wanted me to understand?

How can I respond in a way that I can be proud of where everyone's dignity is acknowledged?

This brings us to apologies: We need a lot more great apologies in our world. Great apologies always include the following: sincerity; acknowledgment of what you did without making excuses or rationalizations, or blaming someone else; and the promise to make amends. Good apologies are transformative because they are a clear acknowledgment of another person's dignity. When you give an apology, especially a difficult or painful one, you have restored your dignity as well, because you have done something worthy of your own self-respect.

On the other hand, fake apologies, the ones where we apologize when we don't mean it, when we just want the other person to stop complaining or being upset with us, usually backfire because we haven't done the work to understand what the problem really is and our part in it. That means we are likely to make the same mistakes, and then the other person rightfully won't trust us. Just imagine a BIPOC speaking out when a friend says a racist comment, and the friend responds with a sarcastic *I'm sorry*. That's not an apology; it's an anti-apology. Anti-apologies are given when people don't have the courage to look at their behavior, accept the feedback they've been given, and want to do better.

Let's do better, even if the other person doesn't say thank you or immediately forgive us. Apologizing is worth it no matter what response you get.

But, we don't want to leave you there. Sometimes what happens after the apology can be almost as difficult as figuring out how to apologize. Below is our advice about how to follow up after you have had one of these messy feedback and apology interactions.

What if I have some feedback for the other person?

Fair question. These things can be two-way streets. For example, you may see that what you did was a problem, but you really may have a problem with the way the person gave you the feedback.

Go back to How Do I Confront Loved Ones (see page 124) and use the strategies we suggest. But basically, say exactly what happened that you didn't like and made you feel like you weren't treated with dignity. State what you would like them to do instead and thank them for hearing you out. Don't repeat yourself and don't give them more than two pieces of feedback to work on.

What if the person I think I offended doesn't say anything? I could be wrong. If I say anything then it will be really awkward. Do I say anything?

Yes, you can! Say: *I may be wrong, but I have a feeling that I offended you/hurt your feelings when I* [the thing you said/did].

If they say: *It's fine.*

You say: *OK, well if I ever do anything that hurts you, please tell me. I'd rather you tell me than not. It's really important to me that you can talk to me about hard things, like when I make a mistake.*

How long should I keep apologizing?

You can't force the other person to accept your apology. A sincere apology given once should be enough. Maybe twice. But, more than that, and it becomes more about your shame and holding something over the person than the apology itself. A sincere apology partnered with a change in behavior is enough.

What if, after I apologize, the person doesn't want to go back to the way it was before?

Forgiveness doesn't mean things have to go back to the way they were before. The person could forgive you and still need to maintain a boundary between you. Being on the receiving end of a boundary like this can be really hard and hurtful. And yet, the path to a better relationship is through acknowledging and honoring that boundary.

What's wrong with wanting some appreciation?

In the summer of 2020, we did two webinars titled "How to Be an Ally." We got a lot of grateful emails after we did them, but we also got some responses from people who disagreed or were upset with something one of us said. One of them was from a Black woman who was offended by something Rosalind said about angry Black women. Rosalind read her email twice—the first time she was defensive. The second time she saw the woman's point. Then she sat with her feelings and wrote a response apologizing and thanked the woman for writing. And then . . . Rosalind caught herself over the next few days looking for an email back from this woman thanking her back for her gracious response. And that's when Rosalind realized she was waiting for this woman's approval that Rosalind's email response proved she "got it" and was one of the good white people. When Rosalind realized what she was doing, there was a lot of laughing at herself and taking the lesson to heart. This woman didn't owe Rosalind a thank you. She didn't owe Rosalind anything. Rosalind had just done the right thing, nothing more and nothing less.

Meditate on It

What was the most difficult feedback someone gave you? Has someone ever given you feedback about something to do with racism?

Ask yourself: What was the most important thing that person wanted me to know?

How can I accept their feedback and show them that I heard them?

KEY TAKEAWAYS

- Getting feedback that you have made a mistake is never easy. It's embarrassing; it makes you feel exposed, vulnerable, angry, defensive, sad, or all these things.

- Give yourself permission to feel these feelings. Remember feelings can pass.

- Apologizing when you have done something wrong transforms relationships for the better. The relationship may not look exactly like you expect or want, but it will be based on dignity.

Why Isn't It All Lives Matter?

KARIN

I have a landscaping company and we work in teams. One day, we were all working in a yard and we were talking about Black Lives Matter and all the protests we were seeing in the news. One of the crew asked everyone, "Why isn't it All Lives Matter? Why are we just focusing on Black Lives Matter?" I don't know if any of us, all being white, had an answer for her. It was so quiet. All of us were figuring out how to answer her question.

SHANTERRA

Do you remember when you first heard the phrase "Black Lives Matter"? Do you remember what you thought or how you felt when you heard it? As a Black woman, I had a couple of thoughts. The first one was, *Wow, I can agree with that!* But, the second thought was, *Wait, really?* That's right,

I questioned a phrase that included me. I know that may sound strange, but I seriously had a moment of *Can I say this? Can I say this out loud and can I say this around white people without making them feel excluded?* I remember thinking about the white people I know—I wondered if they would agree with me when I said Black Lives Matter, or if they would feel like this movement was dismissive of their lives. I also wondered if they would take the time to understand what the movement was about, or if they would feel left out, even though it actually didn't exclude them.

Why was I concerned? Because I worried that if white people became defensive or felt like the movement meant Black people are better than them, instead of the movement meaning bettering Black lives, they would fight to destroy it. Focusing on the idea that the movement doesn't include them would be a perfect way to create a distraction from the real demands. For example, opening grocery stores in marginalized neighborhoods so residents can buy fruits and vegetables instead of processed foods, providing appropriate support for people struggling with mental health and addiction, better training for police, and reform of warrants and court fees.

Can you blame me for being concerned? Throughout history, we see how movements can either bring people together or pull us further apart. The Black Lives Matter rallying cry is not intended to pull us apart from one another. It is shedding light on systemic racism and actively seeking ways to dismantle it. That's it.

The context is often more important than the content.

What's Really Going On

"Why isn't it All Lives Matter?" It's a question that on its face, makes sense. After all, everyone's lives are equally valuable. That's what offering dignity to others is about. "All Lives Matter" speaks to the fear that "Black Lives Matter" is demanding preferential treatment for Black people over everyone else.

But that's not what Black Lives Matter is about at all. It's a lot of things: It's a nonprofit organization, it's a movement, it's a chant that is repeated at protests and marches, and it's a belief.

Here's where our principle comes in: The context is often more important than the content. Content always operates within a context, the circumstances you need to know to fully understand an idea or event. The content here is that everyone's life is equally valuable. The context is what makes Black Lives Matter so powerful. When people respond to Black Lives Matter by saying "All Lives Matter," they are demonstrating an ignorance or a denial of the context we all exist in—namely, that Black lives have never been valued equally to white lives in our culture, institutions, and communities. Even forgetting our shared history of enslavement and segregation, in our more recent past we see disproportionate disciplinary punishment for children in school who are BIPOC, higher incarceration rates of Black and Indigenous people, health disparities, fewer Black people owning homes because of unfair lending practices, and police violence toward Black people, to name only a few. Black people have lived with the repeated message and experience that they are not equal, that their lives aren't as valued as others. So, it's not about Black people wanting their lives to matter *more* than others. It's about Black people wanting their lives to matter *at least as much* as others. It's about Black people wanting proof from systems and institutions that dictate how people move and breathe that their lives matter as much as others. It is about white people acknowledging how Black people have contributed to this country, lived in this country, and survived when our institutions have done so much to make them feel less than.

In this context, All Lives Matter comes across as not caring to recognize this truth, this hurt, and this pain. That's why it isn't a simple, harmless question. That's why if someone is asking this question—if they really want to know the answer—once they know the origins of Black Lives Matter, this context, the resistance to Black Lives Matter and support of All Lives Matter should end.

The cousin of All Lives Matter is the call for Blue Lives Matter, which is then aligned in opposition to calls to *defund the police*. So let's start with what "defund the police" actually means: It calls us to consider alternatives that allow us to divest from policing and invest in housing, health care, education, addiction and mental health treatment, and other vital services that help communities—especially those that have been chronically starved of those human needs—to stay safe and thrive.

When the system works for you, then you naturally think of the police in a positive way. If you are in trouble, they will help you. If you are in danger, they will protect you. But if you are a person of color, and you're in danger and/or you need help, you're constantly evaluating if calling the police will make matters worse.

We are trying hard to not have our words come across as a United States history lesson. At the same time, we should be engaged in a legitimate, significant examination of policing in this country. Yes, of course there are great police officers who are doing wonderful things for their communities. We have worked with many of them, they are our friends and family. But their individual efforts don't take away from the militarization of our police and the unequal enforcement of the law on people of color.

And, it's too easy to solely focus on individual police officers who abuse their power instead of the criminal justice system they operate in that enables them to get away with their behavior. If we are going to say that the context is often more important than the content, then we are obligated to provide some context about the history of policing in the United States:

Although it seems like the police as we know it have always been around, the institution is a relatively new concept. Originally, the "police" were community volunteers; cops were residents and their neighbors looking out for each other.

Wealthy land and business owners hired private security to protect their assets when no official law enforcement existed. This included protecting themselves from the poor or their own workers when they were demanding more pay and safer working conditions, so this type of policing was a class conflict from the beginning.

The first widespread institutional police were the slave patrols in charge of controlling the movement of enslaved Blacks. The patrol system survived emancipation in many states, first informally, and then under the supervision of police forces and organizations such as the Ku Klux Klan.

This police (by any other name) focused on protecting the wealthy's economic resources, and racial segregation became more institutionalized after the Civil War. As formal police forces grew throughout the country, one of their primary responsibilities was to enforce these systems of inequality. From Reconstruction to the Jim Crow laws in the South (and the red-lining and less obvious practices in the North), the police were the weapon to enforce racial segregation.

So basically, from the beginning, the role of police in the United States has been to keep society segregated by race and class. Inevitably, the biases that guided the originators of policing continue to be part of police culture; without a profound reevaluation, how could they not? But the current state of affairs begs some fundamental questions: If the police are here to protect and safeguard "law and order," who are the people and systems that law and order are protecting, and why is so much money spent on policing?

Since 1990, six billion dollars' worth of weapons from the US Department of Defense has been transferred to police departments throughout the country. We are heavily arming our police to fight against our own communities. Why in the world would our police departments need mine-resistant tanks and grenade launchers? Who do they think is the enemy?

Cities in the United States spend one hundred billion dollars of tax money a year on policing—money that could be going to support programs that address the root causes of violence in our communities.

Mass incarceration has been proven to not stop violence. It does, however, sweep the problem out of our public field of vision and makes us feel as if we are getting rid of the problem ("problem," which usually equals Black, Indigenous, and people of color). The mass incarceration of BIPOC helps perpetuate poverty and destroys family stability within their targeted communities.

The bottom line is defunding the police is asking for investment in communities rather than blind investment in the police as we have done so consistently in the past. So, if the idea really bothers you, take a moment to feel your feelings and ask yourself where those feelings are coming from.

Then, go beyond the headlines to do your own research into what that call is really asking for: the right for all our citizens to live in communities free from violence perpetrated by the people representing the law of the state.

THINK ABOUT IT
How do you feel connected to the Black Lives Matter movement if you're not Black?

A Better Approach

What do we say in response to someone defending All Lives Matter? You're going to have to use many of the communication strategies we gave you in the How Do I Confront Loved Ones chapter (see page 124). While keeping in mind the principle that *context is more important than the content*, here are some suggestions for having productive conversations:

You can say: *When these phrases first came out, I realized I needed to educate myself about them. Now I have a sense of what they're about and why people are taking the positions they are. Would you like to hear what I have learned?*

If they say no, you can say: *OK, but if you ever change your mind, I would love to talk about this with you because I am curious about what you're thinking, and I think this issue is really important for people to talk about.*

Then let up. There will be another time.

If they say OK, then you can ask them what their thoughts and feelings are about All Lives

Matter. Show you're genuinely curious about how they got to their opinion. Only after you have heard them out should you share your knowledge, feelings, and thoughts.

If they are listening just to respond and prove to you that you're wrong, you can say,

My bottom line is that all people deserve to be treated with dignity. Can we agree with that as our starting point?

If they won't stop telling you all the reasons why you're wrong, use the strategies in that Loved Ones chapter. Yes, it's going to be frustrating, but this is exactly the scenario we were thinking about when we told you this was going to take practice—you aren't going to do it perfectly every time, but each step you take is worthwhile.

Meditate on It

What does it mean to you to say that Black lives matter?

How would you describe this concept to someone who rejects Black Lives Matter?

How did it feel to read the things we wrote about the police?

KEY TAKEAWAYS

- All lives should matter to our systems and institutions that help us move and breathe easy in society. At present, they don't.

- We must understand our history to understand the challenges we are facing today. That's why context is so essential to understanding the content of what we are dealing with today.

- Black Lives Matter was never meant to imply all lives don't matter. Black Lives Matter is about recognizing the inherent value of a group of people who have been consistently denied that essential right.

EPILOGUE
So Now What Do We Do?

You've officially finished the book, but you may be asking yourself, *What do I do now that I'm done?* Great question. We're going to offer some suggestions, but first, we invite you to just sit a minute and digest what you've read. It was a LOT; we're grateful that you took the time to sit in your own discomfort and we're even more grateful you were courageous enough to do it! We don't take it lightly and you shouldn't either.

Now, you may be feeling ready to take this courageous discomfort out into the world. Here are some ways to put your allyship and advocacy to work.

SUPPORT ORGANIZATIONS THAT END WORKPLACE DISCRIMINATION

You'll remember in the "What's the Harm in Being Curious?" chapter that Black women often have their hair touched, asked about, or even criticized. Many Black women have been denied jobs or positions in our military because of the natural way their hair grows out of their head. Sounds ridiculous, we know, but you can do something to make sure women do not have to endure this discrimination. You can help pass the Crown Act (www.thecrownact.com) in your state if it hasn't passed. The CROWN Act stands for "Creating a Respectful and Open World for Natural Hair" and "is a law that prohibits race-based hair discrimination, which is the denial of employment and educational opportunities because of hair texture or protective hairstyles including braids, locs, twists or bantu knots."

SUPPORT FINANCIAL STABILITY FOR ALL OF US BY SUPPORTING MINORITY WOMEN-OWNED BUSINESSES
Research by Goldman Sachs, the American multinational investment bank and financial services company, has shown that "one of the fastest ways to accelerate change and effectively begin to address the racial wealth gap is to listen to and invest in Black women." That means intentionally looking for and buying from Black women-owned businesses. Many stores, especially online, like Madewell and Target, have started including this distinction for its customers. Also, look up Equality Can't Wait, an initiative launched by Pivotal Ventures, a Melinda French Gates company, to accelerate progress toward gender equality in the United States. They are focused not just on women owning more businesses, but also ending health disparities, closing the education gap, and redistributing political power.

SUPPORT HOUSING JUSTICE
The National Fair Housing Alliance (NFHA)'s mission is to be the voice of fair housing. NFHA works to eliminate housing discrimination and to ensure equal housing opportunity for all people through leadership, education, outreach, membership services, public policy initiatives, community development, advocacy, and enforcement.

SUPPORT CRIMINAL JUSTICE REFORM

The Bail Project combats mass incarceration by disrupting the money bail system—one person at a time. They restore the presumption of innocence, reunite families, and challenge a system that criminalizes race and poverty. They're on a mission to end cash bail and create a more just, equitable, and humane pretrial system. Because bail is returned at the end of a case, donations to The Bail Project National Revolving Bail Fund can be recycled and reused to pay bail two to three times per year, maximizing the impact of every dollar. One hundred percent of online donations are used to bring people home.

Before We Go . . .

There's one more action item we'd like to leave you with. It's simple, and it takes courage to believe. You are needed on this journey. You may never march in a protest or consider yourself on the front lines of ending systemic racism, but you are here, and your presence makes a difference. And you aren't alone. There are many people on this journey with you. There are people waiting for you to speak up.

Many are waiting for you to simply hold space for them and just see them in this world. There will be many opportunities for you to incorporate what you learned, and you are ready for the lessons. Yes, it will be uncomfortable. But continue to take deep breaths and put one foot in front of the other. Besides, you're more courageous than afraid of a little discomfort. You have courageous discomfort!

References

American Bar Association. (March 29, 2021). "Court Fees and Surcharges: Reforms and Post-Pandemic Impact." Americanbar.org. Retrieved February 10, 2022, from https://www.americanbar.org/groups/legal_aid_indigent_defense/indigent_defense_systems_improvement/events-webinars-and-cle-/court-fees-and-surcharges-reforms-and-post-pandemic-impact/

The Bail Project. (January 10, 2022). Retrieved February 10, 2022, from https://bailproject.org/

The Brookings Institution. (January 18, 2022). "Andre M. Perry." Retrieved February 10, 2022, from https://www.brookings.edu/experts/andre-m-perry/

Collins, C. (2018). "What Is White Privilege, Really?" Learning for Justice. Retrieved February 10, 2022, from https://www.learningforjustice.org/magazine/fall-2018/what-is-white-privilege-really

Crenshaw, K. W. (2007). "Framing Affirmative Action." *Michigan Law Review First Impressions* 105, no. 123 (2006). Retrieved February 10, 2022, from http://www.michiganlawreview.org/firstimpressions/vol105/crenshaw.pdf

Davidson College. "Apology for Role in Perpetuating Slavery, Systemic Racism." Retrieved February 11, 2022, from https://www.davidson.edu/about/commission-race-and-slavery/apology-role-perpetuating-slavery-systemic-racism

Equality Can't Wait. (n.d.). Retrieved February 10, 2022, from https://www.equalitycantwait.com/

Goldman Sachs. (n.d.). "One Million Black Women." Retrieved February 10, 2022, from https://www.goldmansachs.com/our-commitments/sustainability/one-million-black-women/

Greenwood Rising. (n.d.). Retrieved February 10, 2022, from https://www.greenwoodrising.org/

Livingston, R. (2021). *The Conversation: How Seeking and Speaking the Truth About Racism Can Radically Transform Individuals and Organizations.* New York: Currency.

National Fair Housing Alliance. (February 7, 2022). Retrieved February 10, 2022, from https://nationalfairhousing.org/

The Official Crown Act. (n.d.). Retrieved February 10, 2022, from https://www.thecrownact.com/

Richter, F. (June 10, 2020). "Infographic: How Much Is the Police's Military Equipment Worth?" Statista Infographics. Retrieved February 10, 2022, from https://www.statista.com/chart/14027/how-much-is-the-polices-military-equipment-worth/

Sarna, J. (January 11, 2021). "The Symbols of Antisemitism in the Capitol Riot." BrandeisNOW. Retrieved February 11, 2022, from https://www.brandeis.edu/now/2021/january/anti-semitism-capitol-riot-sarna.html

Segal, C. (June 7, 2021). "You Can Order Today from These Black-Owned Independent Bookstores." Literary Hub. Retrieved February 10, 2022, from https://lithub.com/you-can-order-today-from-these-black-owned-independent-bookstores/

Steinberg, R. (April 2018). "What If We Ended the Injustice of Bail?" TED Talk. Retrieved February 10, 2022, from https://www.ted.com/talks/robin_steinberg_what_if_we_ended_the_injustice_of_bail?

Urofsky, M. I. (2020). *The Affirmative Action Puzzle: A Living History from Reconstruction to Today.* New York: Pantheon Books.

Wikimedia Foundation. (February 10, 2022). "White Privilege." Wikipedia. Retrieved February 11, 2022, from https://en.wikipedia.org/wiki/White_privilege

Wikimedia Foundation. (February 5, 2022). "Woke." Wikipedia. Retrieved February 11, 2022, from https://en.wikipedia.org/wiki/Woke

Zerkel, M. (October 15, 2020). "6 Reasons Why It's Time to Defund the Police." American Friends Service Committee. Retrieved February 10, 2022, from https://www.afsc.org/blogs/news-and-commentary/6-reasons-why-its-time-to-defund-police

Acknowledgments

We would like to thank our editor Cristina Garces and Chronicle Books for seeing that we could meaningfully contribute to this important topic. Also to Vanessa Dina, Steve Kim, Jessica Ling, Magnolia Molcan, Dena Rayess, Janine Sato, Cynthia Shannon, and Keely Thomas-Menter. To our agent Jim Levine and the LGR agency for watching our webinar and telling us we had a book. We aren't sure we would have thought we could do it if you hadn't seen the potential.

To Esther and Kathy, our mothers, who aren't exactly sure what we do, but constantly encourage us and motivate us to do it anyway! You don't need to know more than that we are your daughters and will always do our best. You give us the room to be ourselves and we are so thankful. We can feel your pride in us.

To Shanterra's dad, Clifford Armstead, who makes sure standing strong doesn't mean standing alone.

To Rosalind's father, Steve Wiseman, and Rosalind's husband, James Edwards, our in-house editors. There was never a turnaround time that you didn't meet. We are so grateful. To James, for telling us to do the webinar that started us down this road in the first place.

To Erin Watley, you are an exceptional reader. Thank you for pushing us in the uncomfortable zone! Your insights and pushback were exactly what we needed. Thank goodness you were there. Also to Bettye Miller, Shasta Clinch, Emilia Thiuri, and Becca Boe.

To the communities around the country who have welcomed us in for the last two decades, even though you knew we would say things that would make things a little uncomfortable (maybe even more than a little uncomfortable). You all are a constant reminder to both of us that people who disagree can still come together and listen to each other. You give us faith and confidence that change is possible to address the pain that so many experience every day.

To Charlie Kuhn, Katie Lowenstein, and Cultures of Dignity for supporting our initial idea and making sure we would be successful.

To the folks who attended that first webinar and who asked really great questions, some of which we incorporated into this book. You didn't know it, but you pushed us, encouraged us, and gave us wings!

To Capitol Reserva, for giving us your time on the never-ending Zoom call! You answered all our questions and were unapologetically yourselves. Your transparency is a gift. Thank you!

To Shanterra's advisor, Margaret Benson-Thompson, who listened and brought out the strength and honesty that was within. Thank you, from both of us.

For every person who disagreed with us, and who made us think more deeply about what we were writing.

To every person who shared their story with us for this book, thank you for trusting us with your truth and for using your voice, even when it was uncomfortable. Your courage is inspiring. We hope we have done you proud.